Create Your Own Job Security

Plan to Start Your Own Business at Midlife

Create Your Own Job Security
Plan to Start Your Own Business at Midlife
by Wm. Hovey Smith

Create Your Own Job Security

Plan to Start Your Own Business at Midlife

Wm. Hovey Smith
A Profit® Book
Whitehall Press-Budget Publications

Preface

As I walked into the head of the Research and Development's Team Leader's office to find out if I was going to lose my job, I felt much as I had when I was running to pull time fuses from beneath a crashed helicopter in 40 below zero weather on the Copper River in Alaska. My heavy arctic gear was thickly encrusted with ice, and every step was more laborious than the one before. Either I would find and pull the second of two fuses I had lit on our spread of explosives or the helicopter crew and I would be blown 100 feet in the air like the ice we were trying to loosen to prevent the loss of the Million Dollar Bridge across the river.

This series of layoffs had been in preparation for months. There had been an agonizing series of interviews and team meetings which among the workers were generally termed, "screw your buddy meetings." The general method was to cut payroll in order to increase profits by reducing the amount of testing on our products. This decision was to be made regardless of longevity in the company or past performance. If one job, once done by three could now be completed by one, the other two people had to go.

Such events had been happening in countless businesses across the world as companies were being downsized, right-sized, or merged with others. These days your replacement might not even be in the same country or even human. The former social contracts between employee and employer are broken, and workers, particularly those in the upper age brackets, need to protect themselves by having an alternative means of preserving their lifestyles.

This book is the first of a series of titles based on the premise that the best way to insure job security is to start your own company. If you are at midlife, you are particularly at risk because of your likely higher-than-average salary and the suspicion that a lesser paid younger person who is more in touch with the present market could do your job.

This brutal logic pays no attention to what you might have done before, but only values what your contribution is to the company's return on investment at the moment. Shortsighted and ill-placed as this logic is, many in this workforce reduction will be in your age group, and perhaps you will be among them.

Create Your Own Job Security will help you discover and examine business opportunities, how to decide which among several possibilities are ideal for you and review the vital steps in starting modern businesses. Among the considerations are: conceiving of a business, selecting the best among several possibilities, writing a business plan, finding start-up money, learning from failure, making mid-course corrections, selecting partners and workers, expanding markets, thinking large potential, and protecting your assets through copyright and patent.

While there are many books about each of the topics that I'm discussing, this book is a comprehensive book designed to jump-start your entrepreneurial future. I pulled that second fuse in time, and I encourage you to light yours as soon as possible to start your businesses while you are still employed and let it burn as you incubate them. This way when you are laid off you can launch your post-50 business with a blast, rather than having to handle the traumas of being laid off and starting from scratch when you are demoralized and can see only darkness and failure.

This is not a one-size-fits-all book. My approach is based on my own experience, and while I believe it is a sound one, there is no formula that will guarantee success. In each chapter there are steps to help you work through a particular issue or advance a particular program. Just as you have a different set of skills, likes, responsibilities, and knowledge; your businesses should reflect all of these and as importantly be something you would do even if no one paid you to do it.

I want to help you discover what that something is, and how you can profit from it. This book is reflective of my longstanding observation that: "There is nothing in human experience that cannot be turned into profit by an inventive mind." In this book I am going to help you discover the potentially profit-making experiences of your life, and how to make businesses out of them that can add financial stability and happiness to your continuing life adventure. If you buy only one business book for yourself or a family member in your entire life, this should be the book.

Chapter 1

Modern Workplace Realities

A look at the whos, the wheres, the whys
and the hows of business today.

∞ ∞ ∞

Almost each day I hear of a new way how workers are being displaced by changes in technology or business models. For example on National Public Radio's Morning Edition there was a program https://www.npr.org/programs/morning-edition/ explaining how once large retail stores were being displaced by smaller storefronts stocked with demonstration products, but there was nothing for sale in the store.

Customers could try out the products in the smaller-format store and order them online for delivery to their door a few days later. Where perhaps 20 workers manned the old-technology retail establishment, only two lesser-skilled salespersons were needed for the smaller storefront.

What's Happening Today

Time was when things were different. I had a cousin, Dean Leonard, who was a decade older than me. He went to Georgia Tech, earned an engineering degree, and after he pulled his two years of service time in the Army, he started work at General Electric in the Jet Engine Division and remained with that company his entire working life. He was a "company man" who might have a reasonable expectation of starting and finishing his working career with the same company.

Dean worked his way up the corporate ladder following a series of in-house company training and advancement programs designed to insure that a maximum amount of his intellectual output was directed towards company activities. It was forbidden, for example, for him to do work outside of the company.

Sure, he could have his hobbies, enjoy aspects of his leisure time, and support charitable causes; but anything that even sniffed of commercial activities was strictly prohibited. The company had bought, paid for and demanded his complete attention. In return they offered health benefits, retirement, challenging working conditions and, implied through the example of his peers, job security.

My Work Experiences

A decade later after obtaining a geology degree, I had a different experience. My choices were to attempt to gain employment with one of the large mining companies as a Mine Geologist or go into the more risky field of exploration geology where I was trying to find and develop new mineral deposits, rather than work extracting old ones.

For the first few years after graduation I worked for an exploration company headquartered in Minnesota, but my work took me to Montana, Texas, Maine and the Carolinas, among other places. When those jobs ran out, I became a Senior Geologist for a company in Tucson and did months-long consulting jobs in Nevada, northern Mexico and Montana as well as worked in Arizona. For a time, I pulled lines and dug holes in the Arizona desert in temperatures that ran over 100 degrees.

Following this I began a nearly decade-long relationship with an Alaskan exploration company and worked in remote areas of Alaska, including on the Alaska Peninsula, the Brooks Range, and several locations in interior Alaska.

None of this did much for my social life. It was only after I returned home to Sandersville did I meet the lady that would become my wife. I had relationships in the past, but these usually ended with a comment like, "What do I need you for? You are never here – always off doing who knows what with whom. Don't bother to call when you get back, I have found someone else." This was exactly the same situation that many in the military were facing. Just as our war vets' spouses and girlfriends were walking away, so were mine.

My work experiences as a contract consultant are typical of today's work environment where a work crew is gathered to do a job and then dispersed when it is over. If you were a good employee you might be called on again and again. If the economic climate changes your job might disappear as quickly as it came. If you have worked in any aspect of the construction industry you know exactly what I am talking about. Specialists, such as those in the nuclear industry, may make very good money indeed; but if no new plants are being built, they need to quickly switch fields.

How You Are Likely to Lose Your Job

Mergers and acquisitions are also facts of everyday life in the corporate world. Very often economies are sought by removing duplicate staffs, closing competing retail outlets and consolidating product lines. This may mean relocating factories from relatively expensive places like New England to the deep South where land prices, workers' wages, and taxes place less of a financial burden on the company.

States are offering very large tax incentives to lure relocating companies to the southern U.S. They may even donate the site and provide a years-long tax holiday after the company opens.

Stay and Lose Your Job or Move

If you don't wish to relocate or can't because of family care responsibilities, you are left in a lurch. If you do not go with the company, there is often no other local work to be had. You are stuck. When you are laid off I want you to be prepared to immediately start your own business to obtain some income after your unemployment runs out. This book is designed to take you through the necessary steps of selecting and starting new business ventures.

Losing Your Job to a Younger Worker

Even if you are willing to relocate, the first to be cut among the company's workforce are those who have risen to administrative and management functions who are in their 50s or older. Your job will be eliminated or you may be replaced by those holding similar jobs in the acquiring company or by younger talent who can bring a more modern skill set to the company at a less expensive rate.

The cruelest cut of all is to scratch you off the payroll just before you become fully vested in the company's retirement program.

There are periodic moves in Congress to make retirement investments portable from company to company, but this has not occurred. The best that can be hoped for is a 401K http://guides.wsj.com/personal-program where you finance/retirement/what-is-a-401k/ invested in a stock portfolio with a portion of their investments being matched by the company.

This account belongs to the employee, even if he is terminated. The company matching part of this 401 K may be of questionable value if it had been in stock that was valued at $50 while you were working but dropped to $5.00 at the time you retired, as was the case with Delta Airlines before they declared bankruptcy in 2005.

Downsizing's Psychological Trauma

Sometimes mergers and their aftereffects may be stewed about for months, which can give you a period of agonizing psychological trauma. An organization that you once regarded as extended family can degrade to a group of cutthroat pirates as each employee seeks to enhance his chances of being retained, at the expense of his fellow workers and perhaps yourself.

Even those who have the power to make the decisions as to who goes and who stays are not immune. One person in the company I worked for was delegated to decide which employees would be terminated to meet a payroll-reduction goal and did what was demanded of him.

He took his own life, apparently over regrets that he saw himself as the person who had ruined what was once a closely-bonded group of friends and coworkers by breaking the social contract between the company and its employees. Knowing the harm he had done, he could not live with himself. More than 1,000 people, including myself, attended his funeral.

Being forced to sign a non-disclosure agreement where you agree not to divulge proprietary company information- https://www.rocketlawyer.com/article/nda-tion or go 101:-what-is-a-non-disclosure-agreement.rl

7

to work for a company competing in the same market is nothing less than a "stab in the back." You have the choice of either accepting the agreement or getting nothing. I am at a loss to think of a polite word to describe such contracts.

This is a huge psychological blow. It implies that the knowledge that you have worked so hard to learn and put into practical application is now worthless. No wonder that you are discouraged about your future job prospects.

Pulling Yourself Out
of Depression and Mourning

For some being "a consultant" is synonymous to being unemployed. For a time that might be so. The challenge is to start marketing yourself either doing something similar to the job that you did with your former employer or taking an altogether different path.

If you are willing to look outside of your immediate experiences in your past job, there are unlimited possibilities of forming a successful company. The task is to select the new venture that best fits your physical abilities, finances, and interests that has a sufficiently large pay-out to fit your needs.

It Happened to Me

It was during such a downsizing event that I lost

my job, although my wife continued to work with the company until she died of pancreatic cancer five years later. During our marriage we had alternated being the breadwinners in the family, as when she had undergone a month-long rehabilitation after a horrific automobile accident.

The One-Person Business

It is no longer necessary for a successful company to have a vertically integrated business where it controls everything from ores coming out of the ground to make metal to selling products in its branded stores, which was the ultimate dream of industrialist such as Henry Ford.

These days a person can run a multi-million dollar business from his own home with a core of three or even fewer people. The necessary functions that were once done within a company may be contracted out, including manufacturing, shipping, fulfillment, and accounting.

Selling Knowledge

It is easier to start a new company if the product you are selling is knowledge. Knowledge, if properly packaged and marketed, is a valuable product. Knowledge brokers include authors, videographers, motivational speakers, and those who might have their university training in the professions, such as engineering, medicine, the sciences, or even the arts. The promotion of causes in the form of non-profit institutions can also bring in significant personal revenue while simultaneously helping your fellow men or the environment.

It is not uncommon for a person who has been with a company long enough to have stored a body of unique knowledge to be offered a contract consulting job for a period of months while he trains his replacements. This may be the first time that he has acted as an independent businessman, even though he was shoe-horned into the position.

If this is you, you may not be all that happy about it. At least it provides some income during a transition period so you can start to change your mindset from being a loyal "company man," to being an entrepreneur.

Store Front Businesses

Conventional store-front businesses are shutting down every day. Although perhaps an intellectually "easy" choice, do you want to be saddled with the added expenses of upkeep, inventory, retail sales, and advertising in order to compete with online sellers who will cut your profits to the point where you must sell at a loss to be competitive? High volume sales are meaningless if every product that goes out the door loses money.

It may be that "hidden costs" that are not directly related to the product will do you in. These might include required health care coverage for employees, increased energy costs, or a sudden rise in the price of your raw materials or shipping.

Overcoming Ingrained Mindsets

Additional mindsets that must also be overcome are related to the union system where each person has a specialized job, and it is a violation of union rules for you to do other work, even though you may have the necessary skills.

This hold-over from the Medieval Guild system is one of the most effective blocks to creative thought that modern society has produced. I am not so much anti-union as I am against thought control.

I warrant that it is far more valuable for a company to have people who can think across traditional job functions, work in other areas as needed and do whatever is necessary to accomplish the task. As a military engineer officer and as a geologist running bush camps in Alaska I often had to compromise and innovate to get things done.

Once at a drill camp where we had only intermittent helicopter support I would take a 10-foot length of drill pipe and walk it over a game trail a half-mile to the drill site when I made my twice daily trips to log the hole so that the drillers could continue work. I also improvised a warm-water shower for the drillers by pumping water into two 25-gallon black-painted drums exposed to 24-hour daylight in a spruce tree.

Business Want Robots and Innovators

Modern companies want individuals who can do more than one function, work productively in multiple areas and are task oriented, rather than only be there to put out their quota of products each day. The repetitive tasks of product assembly, packaging, sorting and shipping are being increasingly automated or sent to lower-wage workers abroad. In modern factories it is not uncommon for night-shift workers to be outnumbered by the security staff.

It is estimated that 30 percent of U.S. jobs are in danger of being replaced by automation during the next 30 years. This puts a large portion of the population at risk of unemployment.

Not only will those over 50 be competing for jobs with their same-age peers, they will be increasingly competing against a younger, periodically unemployed group of individuals who are likely more savvy about modern technology and may have fewer health issues and psychological scars.

These individuals will number in the millions from retail, manufacturing, transportation, and even in the service industries. It is best to position yourself in front of the pack and have your business pulling well in front of this coming onslaught of the knowledgeable unemployed.

Chapter 2

Changing Business Mindsets

How to get your idea across, come up with a plan and convince people what you have really works

∞　∞　∞

If the business models of the Robber Barons of the Victorian Era are no longer practical working models for most people, what do modern businesses look like in terms of how they were formed and operate? These may be divided into three stages, concept, people and execution.

Concept

The human mind in its free state is a stew of ideas that move most freely in that semiconscious condition somewhere between not quite awake and not quite fully asleep or when profoundly fatigued. In this state, I have snatches of songs complete with music come into my head only to largely disappear when I wake. When slightly more constrained by giving it a central thought or theme to work on, the mind can weigh alternatives, make choices and build towards some final objective, although the outcome might be unexpected. This is one way novel thoughts are generated.

New Ideas

Novelty is highly prized as a creative concept, but is not necessarily valued in the commercial world. Whenever it arises, it always has to compete against some established doctrine about how things are done. Only if the idea can be clearly demonstrated to be superior is it likely to progress from concept to testing. This applies equally to intellectual ideas or physical products.

Commonly, the first blush of a new concept is that the originator talked it over with one's spouse, friend, fellow student, or co-worker. If still sounds reasonable it is likely that the originator will want to broach it to some higher authority where eight out of ten new ideas are immediately crushed.

Frequently cited excuses are, "It is not in our product line. This might work, but it would be too expensive. This is good, but who needs it? This concept directly competes against our core business. This is not where the market is going." Equally damming, but not often spoken is, "This was not invented here, or by me, so therefore it can't be any good."

Dust Off Those Old Ideas

Still the baby idea is nurtured in the originator's brain who might also convince a cadre of friends of the soundness of the concept. This is the time to think about forming a company to prosecute the ideas' growth through childhood to launch at some future date as a fully developed adult, or so it is hoped.

If you had experiences like this when you were younger, now that you are in your 50s or older, it is time to dust them off, and see which are still viable. Technological advances may have killed some of them, but possibly some useful spin-offs may remain.

These days it is not unusual for a group of college kids to come up with a concept and from it launch what became a billion dollar company. Silicon Valley is full of such stories. Companies with names such as Google, Facebook, Twitter, and YouTube could have been launched in college dorms. Although of a different generation, you can do the same thing at 50 or even older.

http://www.Google.com
http://www.Facebook.com
http://www.Twitter.com
http://www.YouTube.com

There is no need for an enormous research and development facility with hundreds of employees to conceive of a serviceable product that can solve a problem or improve the human condition and make money for the originator, provided that he also markets it well.

What You Can Do by Yourself

The old model of a person working for years to climb up the corporate ladder is broken. One person using the internet to gather information, experts, coworkers, and raise money can go through these initial steps by himself.

One man is not going to design the next spaceship, but he can use existing information to study the surface of Mars and pick reasonable landing sites and decide what pre-human-landing tests would be needed to verify the results.

Present such a project to NASA, or even a private space company, and he may earn himself a consulting contract. Self-study and some online college classes can get a project like this accomplished. Perhaps you want to start a citizen-scientists study group around this question and set yourself up yourself as the administrator. This work can be done by independent groups. In this era when science budgets are being cut problem-solving thinking can make money for you.

You can become the founding figurehead for any project that you desire and have willing volunteers do most of the work. You can ultimately retire as Founder Emeritus and rest on your accomplishments while the organization that you started continues to carry on after you are long gone.

Our ideas may become immortal, even if we are not. If this sounds like I am talking about a charitable non-profit, I may be. Just because an organization is charitable does not mean that its founder has taken a vow of poverty.

All the large charities started with a single person doing things, gathering a group of like-minded people, conceiving of a workable service concept, raising money, and launching his concept with a local unit and then expanding throughout his state, nation, and perhaps even world-wide. Can you be the person I described?

A Matter of Scale

Once there was a shoe-repair shop, a cobbler, in every community. These were almost invariably owner operated, and he might also have a helper and perhaps an apprentice. This same shop also did leather repair on horse tack and wagon riggings. Unless you live in the Amish Country of Pennsylvania, you are not going to find very many such people today. Shoes have become so inexpensive that it is more cost effective for most people to replace, rather than repair them.

What if your concept was to start a chain of cobbler shops in a section of a nationally branded shoe store? Of the tens of thousands of people who are going to lose their jobs due to automation, there are those who enjoy working with products, building, and reconstructing leather goods. Or maybe the model is to collect the shoes, send them to a central location for repair and return them once they are refurbished.

With modern transportation, perhaps this central repair station might be in Mexico or even India, where skilled leatherworkers can still be found. Most horse tack sold in this country today as well as horse-drawn farming equipment for hobby farmers is now sourced out of the subcontinent. There are those driven by interest and nostalgia, who want to retire and experiment with their romantic versions of early 20th century life and are willing to pay well for the pleasure of doing it.

Another alternative would be that rather than being the maker of the equipment, your function could be to find it and retail it to others. You can become a dedicated supplier to any number of enthusiastic hobbyists in a great number of fields.

Perhaps your original reach was only local, but you can expand to a national level by attending trade shows, franchising your product line to others, and expanding the number of physical outlets Or you could work your entire business from one location using UPS delivery to ship your orders.

Thinking Too Small

When considering a new business most people think too small. Being small is an inevitable state of any start-up, but there should be built-in plans for expanding the business nationwide by increasing the number of physical outlets or, better yet, by working social media to grow your product's distribution.

Even the legal profession has gotten into the act.

Rather than consult your home-town lawyer, you can start your business or write your will using aid from online legal services that can enable you to start a business in any state, regardless of where you live. Legal Zoom.com is one such operation, and there are others.

Say I wanted to start a similar business around the geology profession called for the fun of it, Rock Knockers, LLC. The general plan would be to solicit business from real estate developers to encouraging them to get a geologist to examine a property for potential natural hazards prior to purchasing a property.

When a contract was achieved, a geologist licensed in that state would be identified and brought in to perform the examination to include certain specific evaluations for risks of floods, earthquakes, etc. and perhaps designate portions of the property that should be left as open spaces and parks, rather that used to sprout homes.

Standard evaluation forms could be provided and signed off and sealed by the examining geologist after the work was completed. The geologist, an independent and perhaps one-time contractor, is paid, an administrative fee taken off the top and everyone goes about their business.

Prospecting for Business Ideas

Looking for a workable business idea for an individual is like prospecting for gold. The first thing would be to look at a geological map of the area to see where quartz-bearing granitic or volcanic rocks were found. Knowing that these rock types host gold deposits eliminates a lot of ground that needs to be searched.

The corresponding business concept would be to evaluate the skills and interests of the client. Now the general field of search has been identified, I know that the valuable gold deposits are most likely to be found on the fringes of granitic rocks, rather than in the interiors of massive deposits of granite. This translates to, "What areas of the client's interests are likely to accomplish the financial goals that the client needs? "

Now that the field of search is narrowed, I would do geochemical sampling and gold panning in the streams draining the area to see if I could detect any gold. This will identify a variety of possibilities which need to be systemically evaluated to determine what ones have the greatest potential for success.

The Time Crunch

When positive indications of a gold deposit are found different areas are tested by drilling until the prospector's "paydirt" is found. My business client would now be presented with several possibilities to test to see which are the best suited for his needs and can be accomplished within the time that he has to develop them.

Time, the thing that there can never be more of, is frequently ignored. It takes various amounts of time to start and prosper a business. If you only start thinking about your new business when you are laid off, that time crunch becomes critical. You need money to pay your bills. This demand for immediate cash will likely result in your being forced to take a third-best choice because you do not have the time to develop better opportunities.

Working on your business concept as early as possible while still employed removes the immediate economic pressure and is the approach that I recommend. Don't wait until you are out of work to start prospecting for your own businesses.

People
Getting People with the Knowledge that You Need

As successful, intelligent, and hard-working as you might be, you cannot know everything or do everything equally well. This is why people with different inherent or taught skills have different professions.

If you are going to manage a modern company it is likely that you will require the services of lawyers, accountants, those with manufacturing skills, and someone to distribute, or publicize, your product or services. Very often the first conception of a new idea is overly complex. The inventor may have so much intellectual ownership in his brainchild that he cannot see better ways of doing it. This is when a knowledgeable, detached, individual can spot flaws or perhaps see better approaches to solving a problem than the originator.

Recognizing that other people and knowledge bases are needed to start and work a business, do you hire them or just contract for the services when they are needed? Using virtual corporations does away with office complexes filled with workers and is the way that many modern businesses operate.

There is no longer a need to hire permanent staff when temporary or contracted workers can produce your product or handle the services that you need. Perhaps your packing and shipping can be done by those in a locally funded workshop for the developmentally disabled. Or, there are fulfillment companies that will handle this warehousing and shipping function for you.

Need an artist to design your logo or webpage? There are many available who do this kind of work on a piecemeal basis in nearly every community and will be happy to get the work. You can go online to Fiverr and post a job. Chances are you will www.Fiverr.com find several who will be able to do it for you and, once the initial contact is made, do future work. These workers may be anywhere in the world.

Say you are writing a novel and you need information about a far-away place. Rather than going there, you can hire a researcher in India to discover the details about the city where you have put your character and provide local information on foods, customs, vehicles, etc., that would take you many hours to discover. In short, you do not have to go to Hong Kong to set part of your story in the city. Anytime you need help with anything, there are other people who can be hired to do it.

Sometimes the people that you need may be unrecognized, and literally at your fingertips. These could be your own family, your kid's friends or the guy across the street who loves to tinker with mechanical stuff. If you are open about your needs and talk to people, you can find your temporary help from unexpected sources.

A Personal Example

Having had many interesting hunts with a variety of muzzleloading guns in the U.S., Europe and Africa, I decided to gather my published writings about these hunts, revise them, and republish them in a book. This is the sort of thing that many outdoor writers do.

The problem is that my cut of the outdoor market is so small that I would be fortunate to sell 500 books, which would not pay for the costs of conventional publication. Author House, a print on demand publisher, will publish your book for you and only print copies when orders are received. They also regularly ship to

Amazon.com and other wholesalers and retailers. They charge for each of these services, and one of the major costs was getting the book designed.

What made this book economically viable was that a person I had never met who is also a black-powder shooter and hunter wanted to use some of my content in a publication he was editing for Davide Pedersoli, an Italian maker of replica black-powder guns. I had hunted in Italy with Pierangelo Pedersoli, the company president, and this was one of the segments of my book that he wanted to use, but had no budget to pay for content.

I agreed in exchange my content for his designing the book. Now that the design work was done, at no costs to me, I could, with the aid of a paid ad, publish the book at very low costs, which made its publication possible. This is exactly why you can read **X-Treme Muzzleloading** today. My time was worth more to have this book https://www.amazon.com/X-Treme-Muzzleloading-Dangerous-Smoothbores-Pistols/dp/1477210075 designed than to teach myself how to property lay out the book.

Managing Interpersonal Relationships

In all of our experiences, interpersonal relationships are the most difficult things that we do and the hardest to get right. Relationships with spouses, kids, partners and co-workers can sometimes be challenging to the point of being almost impossible. In a business, non-compatible employees may be reassigned, but there is no such thing as a "child exchange," where an ungovernable child might be swapped for another.

Once you have a cohesive working group that understands each other and the project's objectives, freely sharing thoughts, ideas, concerns, and rewards between them will go far towards everyone working enthusiastically on the project, rather than just putting in their required number of hours at work.

Execution

Starting a business is where most people are stopped cold in their tracks. The danger of failure is so imprinted in their minds that they are paralyzed with fear. They have had the idea of perfection so beat into them through their school training, the concept that failures can be turned into assets is completely foreign to them.

Any new business will have points were things are distressed to the point of collapse. The expected orders do not arrive. The customers do not come. You have built a better mousetrap, but the world is not beating a path to your door.

Modern businesses have learned that failing should be examined and used as a spur to jab the corporate animal into decisive corrective action. Possible corrections are to see if the need for the product is not as strong as it once was because it has been replaced by technology.

A person opened a film-developing business in my small Georgia town, only to close in a short time because film cameras were being almost totally replaced by those using digital technology. Now, those technicians who knew how to do color separations and print three-color images are almost totally gone, and those once common skills only appear in college-level photography classes.

When Technology Changes

When one technology replaces another, there is almost no way to recover except to embrace the new and expand into other markets outside of your traditional work. Regardless of what you do, you have to be watchful about the next trend or market twists that might render your product or service obsolete.

After a period of time, usually about 40 years, the once obsolete may again become trendy as those of that generation seek to recapture something of their youth by possessing something that they always salivated over as a youngster, but could never afford. In this way the old can now become new, and trash can become treasure.

Just as life has evolved, businesses should be thought of as an organic being that must adapt to changing conditions to survive. At 50, one of your tasks in testing a new business venture is to determine where it lies in the midst of changing economic and cultural trends

Chapter 3

How Far and Fast Do You Want to Go

Having an idea is only part of a business
plan. You must plot a course for success.

∞　∞　∞

One measure to use when evaluating a business concept is to establish what your financial and personal goals are, and see which of your potential business opportunities can accomplish them. This sort of choice may have been forced on you in college where you had to declare a major by your sophomore year.

In my case I was torn between archeology and geology, but at that time opportunities in archeology were mostly limited to academics with PhDs competing for a very few positions. Most of the time students were working for free, or even had to pay to work on digs around the world.

In contrast, I had paying work as a geologist while I was still in college, jobs were much more available and the pay was much better. There was still the excitement of making some new discovery which was the core aspect of these professions that appealed to me. I could begin my training at the University of Georgia and then seek additional studies elsewhere, which I did.

This selection led to a full, exciting life, which was not without its ups and downs as the economic market changed, but this choice served me well.

Determining Your Needs

Figuring out what your financial needs are and might be is a daunting task that most people never do. Nonetheless, if you are going to start a business in the hopes of providing financial security you need to know what you are presently spending and for what. Income tax time is an annual event where you have gathered sufficient information about expenses and income to make a realistic attempt to evaluate your financial condition.

You should do the expense side first. Hopefully, you own your home and do not have a mortgage. Otherwise that would be the first thing on your list. Then would come your insurance costs for your health, house, and other properties. Following that would be the usual bills for local taxes and utilities. Now consider what it takes to feed yourself, your family, and pets. Whereas, the other figures were fixed, this cost is less certain, but try the best you can to come up with an accurate figure.

Look back at your receipts and see what your out-of-pocket expenses were for medications and if these will drastically change if you lose your work-provided health insurance. Your pet's medical needs are also a significant expense. Clothing costs should be paired down to just what is needed to replace worn-out garments. Likewise, little or nothing is allocated for entertainment.

I have asked you to ignore your transportation or commute expenses for the moment. These can now be factored in as the amount of driving you expect to do to maintain your household and your vehicle/s.

Total all of this up and see what your expenses have really been and see where they might be reduced. When you have this figure you will have an estimate of the money that is actually needed to support you and your family under the present circumstances. This is likely a conservative estimate, and I would increase it by 10% to allow for the many unaccounted-for expenses that creep into everyday life.

Educational expenses for kids or grandkids are another expense that may have to be cut back considerably or aid sought in the way of grants or work-study for them to continue college. It may be necessary to transfer children to a less expensive institution to keep these costs from breaking the family budget.

Going through this exercise will tell you what income you really need to have your present lifestyle and suggest places where you can cut expenses until you can get yourself reemployed or start producing significant money from your own business.

Post 50 Business Goals
Immediate Income

• Short term income is often the most pressing matter. It helps if you have been prudent and been able to stash away some contingency money, which is usually recommended to be two month's salary that is easily accessible in a savings account or in readily convertible securities. Failing this, the second available pot of money is often a 401(k) retirement program which can be tapped, but at a loss caused by early withdrawal.

Then you can sell other assets, such as boats, cars, property, and finally the home itself. As long as these assets last, they can keep you financially afloat; but this may be only for a matter of months.

• Rental property is a scarce commodity these days, and you will likely be able to rent a spare room to a student or workman along with kitchen privileges to bring in some immediate additional income. If you select your renter carefully, you might have the same tenant for years at the time.

• Earning new income is where your new business venture comes in. If you are lucky, you can take the experiences you already have and start your own company doing basically the same thing.

Say you were in some form of consulting, health, psychological or personal care, you may be able to get your own licenses and start your own practice with some of your previous contacts as your first clients. Often this starts with you working out of your home office, and that may be all that is necessary for the moment.

• Expanding your hobby into a business is another approach. Using the internet to gather a group of similarly-interested individuals you can seek to become an authority in that field who buys and sells products or tools related to that hobby.

There are often trade shows related to any category that you might be interested in that can be used to power-launch your new business and gather clients.

• EBay marketing is another activity that can have a rapid return without much   https://www.ebay.com initial investment. Most likely you will start by using this platform to sell things you already own. Somebody's trash is always someone else's treasure.

Buying trash and selling treasure is always the goal, and bidding on the contents of storage bins may be the way to get started.

• Providing services to local residents can keep start-up expenses small, permit you work out of your house and let you bond with your neighbors. This can be in the way of a personal shopper for those who are elderly or too busy to take time to do these things themselves. This activity might also be pet care or car maintenance. Any teen-aged at-home resident or non-working spouse might also participate.

• Commission sales can be profitable provided the sales potential and market area is sufficiently large to support your activity. The amount of return you will receive is directly related to the personal energy that you are willing to put into the product that you are pushing.

Some sales plans are as much scam as businesses with a few being little more than Ponzi schemes which depends more on extracting money from other potential members of the sales organization than returning income from the products that are sold.

Intermediate Term Income Possibilities

• Knowledge as a salable commodity is frequently overlooked by many in considering a new business. All consultants in health, business, or finance are basically selling knowledge. Everyone has a certain store of knowledge that could be of value to someone else.

This might be life experiences, some body of knowledge accumulated in an academic setting, or something that was derived independently. Transmissions of this knowledge can be done on a one-on-one basis, through social media, in books, seminars, white papers, and through commercial radio or TV.

If you have the ability to write and speak well, you

can sell what life has taught you to others. Often the first building block of this approach is a book which gives the author a degree of credibility, access to the media, and ultimately national exposure, provided that the author promotes himself aggressively. A book without sufficient promotional outreach is not sufficient to sell you as an authority.

• Royalties and other rights to creative products can provide long term continuous income without you having to be physically involved with making and selling products. This is like owning a rental property, but without having to pay taxes and upkeep.

The authorship of books, plays, TV, and movie scripts can provide significant income provided they are commercially successful. This is a very competitive field and many fail, but if a person has sufficient drive they can be successful.

Long Term Income Possibilities

• Selling your own branded products usually takes more time and expenses to design, legally protect, and make the products than any of the foregoing. There are more risks because more start-up capital is needed. Sometimes partners and/or investors will be needed to carry off a successful venture. New products do have a certain appeal, but if not linked with effective marketing will almost invariably fail.

• Store-front businesses are what come to most people's minds when they think about starting a new business, but doing this successfully takes much more market research than almost anything else.

A better plan for success is to first start in your own home, and only when your business needs demand an enlarged facility do you open a store. In many cases this may never be necessary even though your business may bring in millions of dollars in sales.

• Founding a non-profit service activity to fill a community need will require a strong statement of purpose, a governing board of respected individuals, state licensing and a sufficiently large population to be served to justify the venture. A portion of the operating revenue may come from State and/or Federal funds secured by the successful completion of a competitive grant-writing process.

It helps if the founder has professional credentials, is associated with academic or religious organizations, and is well-published in his field. If you are not, gather people around you who are.

Business as a Social Function

Starting a business requires a considerable investment in time, and as you age you will come to the realization that time and the energy that you have to do things are the most important things that you possess. This time-energy relationship may become so significant that you do not want to do the full-blown effort that is required to produce large amounts of cash, but are willing to settle for less income in exchange for less stress and more interaction with society.

In this case the business becomes more of an enhanced hobby, such as many craftspeople do who participate in local and national crafts fairs. If managed correctly crafting may pay expenses, but most often is a break-even or money-losing proposition. A better business model is to sell to craftspeople and teach the crafts rather than make them yourself, other than demonstration pieces.

If you do not have the interests or talents to produce craft items, there is in every community a need for small engine repair and service people where the items are brought to you and a fee charged to repair them. Even in today's throw-away society there are times when it is better to fix an item than junk it, and it is certainly a more ecologically friendly process.

This is one way that a person can compete with big-box stores, because they depend so much on low-margin retail that repairing items is such a marginal profit producer that they are not interested. If you come to know the store manager, they might even give you referrals.

Running a perpetual flea market has been a revenue producer for many non-profit organizations who collect money from the exhibitors for booth space. This can also be done by private individuals who happen to own property near major highways, although zoning restrictions may prohibit such roadside activities which are often unsightly. These activities are now moving indoors into abandoned malls, which closed because they could not compete with online sales.

Vendors going into high-cost spaces must push high-value products in order to pay the rent, and only major metropolitan areas typically have sufficient traffic to justify mall conversions. To be successful these vendors should also have a large online presence, so they are not totally dependent on foot traffic. In most cases it is better to specialize in a particular type of product, rather than attempt to be too much of a generalist.

Purchasing a former mall and leasing space may be a way to get revenue from businesses like used bookstores, vinyl record shops, used clothing outlets and hobby shops that often repopulate former malls, provided that the space is reasonably priced.

Along with these shops there are often specialty food markets which sometimes incorporate food-service areas in the backs of their establishments. These combined stores-eateries require considerable capital to get started, pass food-inspection and serving standards and an experienced staff to run. Very often these are started and popularized by immigrant communities, although they may become permanent fixtures manned by several generations of a family.

Perhaps the concept of doing a mall conversion appeals to you as a way to help bring life back into a blighted community, but you lack the cash to make it happen. However, this is something that any individual can bring to the attention of the local city government and if pushed successfully, perhaps the venture capital can be raised from State and Federal resources and you may become a manager or participant in the project without having to fund the venture yourself. One person's vision can revitalize an entire community if it can be brought to fruition.

Chapter 4

Conceiving Your Million-Dollar Business

Get out of your own way and make that business happen. No one is going to do it for you.

∞　∞　∞

If you have the drive and stamina for it, it takes the same amount of energy to start a business with a million-dollar sales potential as it does to start a small one, so you might as well go for something that has real potential, rather than self-limiting yourself to smaller-scale activities.

The trick is to discover what that business might be, and the first step is to overcome the notion that you cannot possibly succeed, so there is no reason to make the attempt. In short, get out of your own way.

What your objective is at this stage is to accumulate a list of at least 10 and preferably more like 25 different potential business opportunities so that you will be able to implement one or more of them to fill your needs. You will later sort these by short-term, medium-term and long-term possibilities.

It is likely that you will start with something that is relatively easy and will produce quick income while you are simultaneously working on other projects that will take time, extra training, or people to accomplish.

This way you will be able to gather experience and gain confidence before you take the plunge to go after your million-dollar hit.

Finding Potentially Successful Business Concepts

• Look around your immediate environment. Most people go through life busy with tasks, duties, and entertainments and do not really observe life. They are too busy rushing about to see viable business opportunities that are in front of them.

Pay attention to people who are having difficulties and see how you can help them have an easier life by providing a service that they are willing to buy. Things like being a personal shopper or house cleaner come immediately to mind, but look beyond that.

Can you, for example, start a business by hiring vetted individuals to provide such services for others and build up a series of clients? By building a service base in a metropolitan area, you can expand first into the at-home market in neighborhoods and later into cleaning businesses, as your company gains a reputation for providing dependable service.

After having expanded throughout one metro area, you can franchise your business in other cities. Uber started just this way and then went national and international.

• Identify working models and adopt or adapt them. If you visit another city or country and see something that is working there that you do not have a home, see if that service or product can be successfully introduced back home. Oftentimes, small tweaks will be needed to make it salable, but if these can be teased out something of real value can result.

• Profit from other business' failures. Most small start-up businesses fail. Most of the time it is because of competition from lower-priced mass-market stores, online sales, failure to market their product or idea successfully, lack of capital, becoming obsolete because of technology or failure to fully understand their market's needs.

If the business interests you, do an objective analysis and discover what caused the business to go under. To be sure the founder was full of enthusiasm and hope at the start, but what did him in? Was it lack of marketing? Was it that he thought too small? Was it a bad location? Was his product outreach too small? Was there a better competitor in that marketplace?

What? What? What?

If the "Whats" can be identified and resolved, you may be able to take that failed business, purchase its assets at give-away prices and turn it into a profitable venture. You might even bring in the founder or workers back into the new venture if they are not so demoralized as to no longer be of use.

Putting money into a failing business is a very risky activity unless the reasons for the business' poor returns can be positively identified and corrected.

If the business' owner can only think of doing the same thing the same way, additional money will only prolong the agony, lose time and likely not avoid going bankrupt. Regrettably, the prudent thing to do is to let the business fail, reorganize. and start fresh with new management, new techniques, and new marketing. That is a hard lesson to learn because so much human ego is involved.

• New concepts. There is a line of thought that goes like, "There is nothing really new in the world, only adaptations of what is already known." I take comfort and disappointment in this statement. The comforting aspect is that if one can become sufficiently steeped in human knowledge there will always be found a key from which to derive something new.

I am disappointed in that this statement dismisses the possibility of anything being derived that is totally new, which is a self-limiting restraint on human progress.

Periodically there have been cultures that decided that everything worthwhile was already known, so that no additional knowledge from outside that culture was wanted or desired. This was true of both China and Japan and of Isis today. During the industrial age in England there was even a move to close the patent office because "everything worth having had already been patented."

I would like to affirm that there is the new and the yet to be discovered in all aspects of human activities, although we can only understand it in light of present knowledge. This gives you the right to think and discover some new business concepts, adaptations of methods or thoughts from which to springboard a business that has enormous profit potential.

These new thoughts, however outlandish appearing, also need to be on your list of potential businesses. Can you, for example, make us nearly immortal? This brings up the follow-up question, "Do we really want to live for centuries, and what kind of life would that be?"

These are philosophical questions of merit which need to be answered before we are propelled unknowingly into a future where human lives can be indefinitely prolonged, but is the quality of that life diminished to the point of being unacceptable?

Millions of dollars have been, and will be, spent trying to resolve the technical and philosophical questions revolving around this issue. Often science fiction writers are the first to confront these issues, expose them to alternative examinations and only later does fiction become fact.

Technology is reducing that time-gap. In the days

of Jules Verne there was a hundred years from the time he wrote of going to the moon and undersea craft until they were achieved. Now that gap may only be years or decades.

• Experiences from work. Your past series of jobs have likely been many and varied. List what these have been, and think about what you did and learned.

Can any of the tasks that you once did manually now be successfully aided by some new methods, thoughts, or technologies? Did you once have a good idea that no one would listen to? If so drag these out, frame them in terms of business opportunities and add them you your list.

• Learn from co-workers. In any work environment you were surrounded by people who were doing other things. Did they have any particular techniques or thoughts that would be useful in a broader context? Do these have business applications?

Uncovering these things from decades past can be done by retrieving physical objects, reviewing news clippings and sorting through old reports. While this sounds like a visit through "memory lane," and a waste of time, it is not.

If you worked for a company for 20 years, it is certainly worth two solid days going through these materials and seeing what might be retrieved. If you come up with nothing, then set that material aside and look at it again at a later time.

There are things of potential value in anyone's two decades of life. You were just not mentally ready to recognize them. If so, it will be helpful to have a friend, spouse or child go through them with you; because they may see something significant that you discounted because of overfamiliarity.

• Look outside of your field. Modern schooling and regimentation have restricted many people to only considering business opportunities that are connected to their past professional employments.

This is a shortsighted and self-defeating approach. Consider other areas in which you are interested and attend professional conferences and activities where people of diverse interests and activities are gathered.

Even if you do not attend conferences, things like the radio broadcast of TEDx talks, audio and video learning, such as The Great Courses series, can expand your intellectual   https://www.ted.com/watch/tedx-talks
interests and sug-   https://www.thegreatcourses.com/
gest business opportunities.

• Reconnect with school and college chums. You made many human contacts during your school and college years, and if the opportunity exists to reconnect with them do so.

They and you shared unique experiences and their

subsequent lives may well provoke business concepts and suggest partnerships that might be beneficial to you both.

Did you and your friends once talk about some futuristic notion that seemed impossible at the time, but which is now practical? Not only will this communication revive a once-significant comradeship, it can also yield valuable ideas.

• Check on your students. If you were a teacher or taught classes in an industrial or military setting, you might be able to reconnect with some of your former students who have now progressed in the business world.

The exchange of intergenerational knowledge is of value in exposing you to things that might not have been significant to you, but are of great importance to younger generations. Take the attitude that, "There is no one that I cannot learn something from or teach something to."

• Listen to strangers. Chance conversations with a seatmate on an airplane trip can sometimes yield important information about market trends and in areas where you have had little experience can provoke thought in different directions.

Random or chance activities are vital to almost every statistically-based study. It should not be surprising that randomness also works in considering business opportunities. Some, when looking back on how they came to start their successful businesses, might call such contacts "Fate," but it is as much chance as anything. If you can and will communicate with others, some very good things can result.

Sorting Through
Your Business Concepts

By this time you have accumulated a list of potential business activities, and it is time to combine the goals that you set in a previous chapter with other factors to decide which businesses are the best fit with your present knowledge base, experiences, health, and financial resources.

Any list should include short-term, medium-term, and longer-term business concepts. If all fall into one category, you need to rethink and expand your list before you start sorting. What you want at this stage is the largest possible list, because you will likely want to consider several business opportunities in sequence to fit your financial needs.

Short-term business concepts

These may be one or several activities that might be used generate immediate income. Most do not think of these as business ventures, but they are.

These might include selling seldom used or duplicated items to raise immediate cash. Such things might be done on consignment, although eBay sales can often be more profitable because you are appealing to a wider market. If the bid price does not meet your minimum, you can withdraw the item. Direct sales between you and a customer will always have a larger return than working through an intermediary.

Anyone of any age can engage in selling products, but know your market, learn how to present your products with good photos, research past selling prices, and don't be blindsided into unrealistically pricing your items. Often you will be able to obtain at least 25% more for an item through selling it yourself and using others to accomplish the same task.

Speculation in something like the stock market or Bitcoin should be avoided at this stage, because the money you have is http://money.cnn.com/infographic/ going to be needed technology/what-is-bitcoin/ to pay bills and meet unexpected expenses such as car repair or doctor's visits. If your needs for additional income are not too large, eBay selling might be sufficient to accomplish your aims of generating extra cash as it is needed.

Medium-term business concepts

This group of concepts requires extra development that might include taking classes either online or at a community college, getting state certification or licensing for your profession, or obtaining needed equipment to set up a shop.

Be patient and shop around for the best deals on whatever you need. You have time, and not everything has to be obtained "right now" with the added costs of higher-priced shipping. Sort through your possibilities and rank them according to the amount of additional work that you have to do in order to launch that particular business. That work should include considerations of the amount of time that you need to invest as well as the amount of money that will be required.

Did your termination agreement give you the option of engaging in some free training or is there any program that you can sign-up for from the State or Federal governments? There may be, particularly if your job loss resulted from competition from less expensive foreign imports or if the work you did has been exported to another country.

If you still have educational benefits available under the G.I. bill, seek those out. These do not expire and are available to you until they are used. Between the State Employment Office and the Veterans Administration, there may be programs than can benefit you. Some creative activities like writing magazine articles, blog postings, website building, and making videos also fall into this category.

https://firstsiteguide.com/what-is-blog/

You will benefit enormously from developing an effective online presence to broadcast your thoughts and activities throughout the world. If you do not have these skills, this is the time to develop them.

Long-term business Prospects

These are concepts that may be months or years in the future. They might include real-estate investments, relocating to another part of the country or starting your own limited liability company. Often these might involve raising capital or seeking a partner, both of which should be done only after the business concept is well thought out, and, literally, ready to take to the bank.

Such a move will require a strong commitment from you on your time and resources. If you are confident in your concept, but do not have the skills or will to successfully manage it yourself, then you will need to convince others to join you in this venture to supply the needed personal capital to make your business a success. This is not the place for half-hearted efforts. Once launched, this effort has to be all or nothing if it is to have a chance of success.

If the business stumbles during its early stages, the company officers need to have the ability to analyze what went wrong, correct it, and charge ahead.

If you don't want partners, don't want the bother of shipping product, and have the need to control the entire effort yourself, some of the creative arts, like book or screen-play writing may be your preferred outlet. Many writers prefer an introspective life, while others need outside stimulations to perfect their work. In either case writing is best learned from doing it. You must put words on paper, even if you must dictate them for someone else to transcribe.

Best-selling authors have often written for decades, but new writers with the proper coaching can also be successful. If you have a book in you that can satisfy some societal need or tells a gripping story, you can become a successful author. Imagination is something that what we all have and if properly stretched, exercised, and perfected can lead to a successful result producing fiction or non-fiction books.

Ranking Your Business Concepts

Once you have your list of perhaps 20 concepts you can categorize them into the short, medium and long-term groups that I just described. Don't bother to attempt to further categorize them at the moment – just get them into these categories on separate pieces of paper.

Short

Start with your short-term possibilities. Some of these will likely have to do with raising immediate income. Move this group up to the top of the list. Others may require you to invest money in the project. Move these to the bottom of the list. The money-neutral group can remain in the middle.

Now consider time. Which can you do more quickly than the others? While keeping them in the list subgroups that you have established, move those that you can accomplished more quickly up in the rankings.

Within the subgroups, which ones will return the most money in the shortest time? Move these up in your rankings. Your sheet of paper is likely getting very messy at this stage so either re-write it or list the possibilities on cards that you are shuffling in a pack. If you do cards, still put their current numerical ranking on a corner.

As you re-write the list consider desirability. Answer the questions, "Do I really want to do this now?" and "Am I going to regret this for the rest of my life?" If the answers are respectively, "No" and "Yes," remove that card from the remainder of the stack and re-order the remainder. You may have to revisit selling Grandma's silver later, but for the moment there are other things that you can do first.

Once you are satisfied that you have made the decisions as to what you can do to with your Short Term Business Concepts, systematically execute them. It is all too easy to become so involved with the planning of your future life, that you overlook the vital steps of putting your Short Term concepts into place. Once you get cash in hand, if that is your goal, then considering your Medium Term Concepts.

Medium

The initial rankings are done in the same way as you did for the short-term category, but additional steps are needed because of the more complex and often physical nature of the concepts. Consider them as you did before, rank those higher that can produce income more quickly than the others, and again consider the personal desirability of the concept to you.

This desirability should also include your physical ability to do the tasks needed to make this venture go. It may be that something you want to do is going to require some physical conditioning or training.

Now the desirability question becomes, "Is this something that I really want to do for the rest of my life, or will this keep me solvent while I continue to work on what I really want to do?" A practical example of this is the playwright who waits tables while he is flogging his play to New York agents and producers.

Other considerations are the needs for additional training in formal or informal settings, acquiring needed tools, finding a potential collaborator, or raising money for your project, compared to getting enough money to survive on a daily basis.

These things will take some time, perhaps months,

to put into place. In the meantime you should also be taking positive steps to put yourself in better physical condition than you are now. This conditioning will pay off in improvements in your mental and physical state.

Those business possibilities that you can do in the shortest time get put higher on the list. Whereas your Short Term List might include several things that you can do to meet your immediate needs, the Medium Term List now requires you to make some decisions as to which two of perhaps six options do you really want to go after.

You cannot do everything, so it is time to make some choices. Available money may make the decision for you. However, try to hold out for what you are really passionate about.

The reason that passion is more significant than absolute monetary return is that without passion your business efforts will be self-defeating, and you are likely to quickly lose interest in driving your entrepreneurial venture forward.

If you are reading this book you have already had more than enough, "doing what is needed to get a paycheck into the house." Now you have the opportunity to do something that you really want to do, rather than work at what you had to do. Have the courage to make that choice.

With this category of potential ventures you are moving from sheets of paper and cards to folders that will be needed to contain your concepts, the certificates of training that you have received and the contacts that you have made.

Computer files are handy and portable, but you will also have physical objects that need to be retained. Papers have the attributes that they can be physically sorted and reordered which is not so handy to do with computer systems unless you have side-by-side units.

Long

It is entirely possible that as you gain more experience, training and put more work into one of your Medium Term Concepts that it will evolve into this Long Term Category. Again, go through the sorting methods that were previously described, but now you are going to be restricted to only selecting one category from the group.

This is a hard, but necessary, discipline. The selection process may take place over a period of years and could evolve into one concept being tried and replaced by another. In this category extra training is almost always required, and partners may have to be brought in to provide skills that you do not possess. Limited scale production facilities may have to be built, contracts made, production schedules met, and payrolls established.

Running a business, rather than fanaticizing about it, includes the steps of planning, prototyping, production, marketing, sales, distribution, collection, accounting, and gathering personnel. Even if you have an intellectual concept, such as book writing, all of these steps have to be met if your book is to be successful.

Business is business. If you do not think that what you are doing, even if it is in the arts, is not a business; think again.

Materials related to these concepts are best held in 2-inch binders until these are outgrown and one must go to file cabinets. Modern technology and methods, which will be discussed later, can help considerably in reducing the amount of paper and things that you must handle.

These space and things obstacles can be overcome once your business becomes large enough to arrange to contract out services like accounting, payroll, distribution, etc. Or, if you are somewhat smart about it, all of these functions can be given to the manufacturer that you sell your invention to, to the on-demand printer who does your books, to the production company that presents your play, or the distributor who sells your yard-art designs.

Chapter 5

Identifying Your Target Customers

Who will buy what you are selling? How are you going to reach them?

∞   ∞   ∞

With a few business concepts in hand, "Who are your intended customers?" Before you can determine where your potential customers are, you need to discover who they are. Who is going to buy your widgets, books or ideas? How do you find out?

Discovering your Audience

Using the term audience, instead of the more customary "customer base," reinforces the concept that you are marketing whatever you do to real people, not robotic algorithms. Identifying these people and gathering mailing lists is your first task after you have finalized your product.

Even before you produce it, you will need to know who is in your potential market group. It is easy for inventors to be so caught up with the thrill of invention to overlook the user. This applies to hard goods, software, books, plays, and artworks. The term "user friendly" is commonly applied to almost everything these days, whether it is true or not.

With a large enough market population, anything, no matter how perverse or twisted the concept may be, will appeal to someone. But, are those someones numerous enough and do they have the buying power to support your product or activity? How can you find out?

One of the first things is to research who is doing, or has done, something similar, and were those efforts successful? If I write a play for Broadway about an axe murderer who chops up his victims and sells them as meat pies out of his shop, will it sell?

Sweeny Todd had successful runs in New York and elsewhere with one production even selling meat pies to the audience. If even that gruesome concept can fly as entertainment, what is off limits? Anything? If approached in the correct way and if production values are good, almost any concept can be examined in the form of a Broadway play, such as the unlikely story of The Best Little Whore House in Texas. This was not only a successful musical, it also made a delightful movie starring Dolly Pardon and Bert Reynolds.

Who do You Know?

Family, friends, business acquaintances, fellow church members, LinkedIn associates, and Facebook followers may be the first groups that you approach. Likely your first sales will be to people that you already know well.

While sales are sales, the possibilities offered by selling only to those that you personally know are limited. See if you can expand your market by approaching groups that these people are associated with. Lions Clubs, for example, are often looking for speakers. This local-approach effort might also include participating in local crafts fairs, clubs, school money-raising events, or social happenings, such as book signings.

Sometimes your status in the community will allow you to garner local sponsorship for an event or to put on a play. If it is knowledge that you are selling, local community college branches or even prisons may be willing to pay you to teach classes on developing life skills, communication, the arts, or trades.

Your possibilities for this personal outreach approach can be considerably enlarged if you live in a large metro area and maybe just your in-city contacts may be sufficient. However, if you are going to be really successful you need to locate potential customers who live in what will become your regional, national, and international markets. What are these customers like, and how can you best appeal to them?

Learning About Customers You Have Never Met

One of the advantages of making personal sales is that you have a chance to see who your customers are. You can learn about their age, sex, economic status, and likes/dislikes about your product.

To what groups do they belong? What books do they read, and what TV programs do they watch? Do they go to high-end houseware fairs? Maybe they really like NASCAR racing. Nearly everyone will tend to gravitate towards some organizations of like-minded individuals. If you can identify these groups you can devise a strategy to approach them through free offers or reduced-price promotions to get their names on your Email lists.

If you are providing a service, you can have a free or very-low-priced consultation – the equivalent of test driving a car. Perhaps you can do a white paper examining one aspect of marketing which will provide some exciting new approaches while offering, for a fee, directed online mentorship or even on-site consultations about their businesses. The real objective is to build your list so you have an ever-increasing population of potential customers who know you that might use your product.

Every major organization has an annual meeting. At these meetings there are often associated trade shows where exhibitors may buy booth space to shill their products. This is an excellent way to meet people, talk about your products and collect business cards and Email addresses to expand your mailing lists.

It is more effective to collect an address for a later email campaign than handing someone a booklet at these events. The booklets will very often be politely accepted and then discarded or put into a pile to be looked at later, but that later never arrives. If someone takes the time to write their name on a pad, that means that they are interested. You will collect fewer names, but those few will be the ones that will more likely purchase something from you.

Make Your Own Focus Groups

Focus groups are usually composed of participants who hear a pitch about a product and provide unbiased input about what they think about the concept. Such inputs are valuable in product design, but another bit of information from such groups is finding what age group and social demographic is most likely to buy what you sell.

Another valuable insight can be how to package your product to appeal to different segments of the population. This packaging can be physical, visual or auditory. Knowing, for example, that the age group you are shooting for uses Google Search to help solve their everyday problems and particularly likes YouTube videos can tell you that you need to make videos. Similarly, others may prefer their information come from talk radio. In this case https://www.thepodcasthost.com/ listeners-guide/what-is-a-podcast/ you need to appear on large market Podcast talk radio programs.

To get value from focus groups you must be able to disassociate yourself from your product long enough to be able to hear damning information without being defensive. You must be willing to listen to what your focus groups have to say and take constructive action. While it is always ego-stroking to hear good things about your product or activity, you must be able to also hear less favorable comments, recognize the criticisms that are valid, and correct them.

To enlarge your sample population you can present your product online, offer a reward for a written response, evaluate your results and add the people who responded to your mailing lists. This way you can not only generate your own diverse Focus Group, you will also built a base for future sales.

Although not often seen that way, blogs and product dedicated Facebook pages can also act as product input mechanisms to serve many of the same functions as focus groups without putting a group of people in the same room to answer a formal questioner.

Commercial Marketing Lists

There are companies who will sell you mailing lists for geographic areas. You can decide that you want to market to single men who buy books that are between 45 and 63 who make more than $100,000 a year in the Chicago metro area. You will pay X dollars per thousand names and may get a 1 to .01 percent positive response rate.

Unless you are selling a high-ticket item like real

estate, this low response rate will likely not return your investment. Deriving your own lists will result in a much higher response rate than making a blind stab with a prepackaged product.

Chapter 6

Selecting Your Best Business Model

Have a plan. Know what you want to do before you start.

∞ ∞ ∞

After spending decades in the corporate world with a mind-numbing commute to work, fighting to get into your designated parking place, riding up a germ-infested elevator, dodging the cleaning crew while you are balancing a cup of coffee that you paid too much for, and clamoring over some else's waste-paper basket to get into your cubical, you probably want a change.

Maybe your vision of a business is running it from your bed while you look out over a green of a New Zealand valley to the blue Pacific below.

Perhaps it is to have your office in a separate room off your house so you work in your PJs in the comfortable surroundings of your books, easy chair and computer with an exercise machine in the corner, which is exactly what I do. No commute, no traffic, no harassing boss, no inconsiderate co-workers, and no interrupting your work to go to meaningless meetings or trainings.

This business can be you in your own house with

your family, pets, land and sporting activities at your fingertips. Nothing you really need to do is more than 200 yards away. Think how productive you can be without the distractions of the typical work environment. No wonder that you can get things done, do complex tasks, learn things, and do more than ever before. There are no more productive individuals that those who can work by themselves.

That's me. That is my business model. It may not work for you. You may be a person who thrives in the midst of a major metro area. You need to be where the action is if you want to make movies that may cost tens of millions of dollars to film, may employ hundreds of extras as well as editors, videographers, sound people, music producers, and special effects guys/gals. That location was once Hollywood, but other movie-production locations, like Atlanta, have become increasingly important.

If this is the sea in which you wish to swim, you obviously have a different outlook on life than I do. There is nothing right or wrong with either model or using them both at different parts of the creative process. As a screenwriter you may need to work in absolute solitude to get your vision on paper, but during production you are immersed in a seething mass of humanity.

Now that you are in mid-life or older, you have been in situations where, "I never want to do that again." Which is contrasted with, "That was fun. I want to do that some more." Now with your own business you have the opportunity to be in complete control. With your destiny in your hands, do you have the foresight to visualize it and the willingness to act?

Owner-Operator

It is very often true that, "There are no people who work harder than those who work for themselves." Authors are, by nature, often solitary individuals who largely produce their own products. An extreme example was an author who wrote on a linotype machine setting type so that when he was done, all that he needed to do was to use his plates to print his book. Computers are today's linotypes whose electrons have taken the place of liquid lead once poured into type fonts to make book pages.

It is now possible for an author to write, edit, design, and produce his E-book for distribution throughout the world through sources like Amazon.com. The scores of people once required to get this done are no longer needed. Soft cover and hard cover books can be printed and shipped on demand so a writer no longer has rooms filled with boxes of unsold books that he has to package and ship.

An inventor can likewise have a small shop where he can produce prototype products in order to secure his patents and demonstrate them to potential buyers who can put his ideas into production. This way he can avoid the numerous problems and legal hurtles of setting up a factory.

Even if he wishes to control the marketing of his product, he can contract production out to other sources while he handles the shipping and billing. Or, even the fulfillment part of the business can be done under contract. Today's inventor can remain an independent business operator with all of the other functions of his business contracted out to others.

Partnerships

Having a partner and collaborating with them can work provided:

• You have the same vision of the product's end results.

• You can respect each other's talents and skills.

• You have complementary skills. Although your skills may overlap in some areas, in others your partner is much more skilled that you are.

• You can communicate on a regular basis. There were in the Victorian Era partners' desks where one person sat on one side and the other was directly across, so if they needed to speak all they had to do was to open their mouths.

• You equally commit to the project. If one partner feels he has to carry the lion's share of the load, this becomes mentally and psychologically burdensome.

• You share a sufficient number of interests and views that non-business-related conflicts do not detract from your joint efforts.

• You have a firm financial agreement as to how costs and revenues are to be divided.

• You share responsibilities for needed housekeeping chores.

• You have some method of jointly sharing work files.

• You are close, but not so dependent on each other that nothing can be done unless you both are present.

• You can take constructive criticism from your partner and build on it.

• You can take advantage of and build on each other's life experiences.

• Working together is an enjoyable, fun experience where you look forward to each day's work and seeing what you can accomplish together.

If this list sounds much like what you would be looking for in a spouse, that is not far off the mark. Of course the sexual component is missing unless your partner is also your spouse. This can, and has worked, for many start-up businesses.

With spouse-partners the challenge is to make reasonable accommodations between your private lives and work. In any event the spouse has to be accepting and hopefully supportive of this new arrangement with a stranger who has now become a significant part of their lives.

A well-functioning partnership is one of the most difficult of life's challenges. A model from the past was that the family-owned business would take in a son or daughter at a very junior level and then as the parent aged the younger members of the family would work up to the level of being partners in the firm.

Cultural diversity can be an asset in this globally-connected world, and your partner may be a different race or sex and have a vastly different life experience. These differences can be significantly important in the design and marketing of the product.

English has become the language of international business, and it is no longer out of the question to have significant arrangement with partners or co-workers in Europe or Asia.

One of the hallmarks of a modern business is that you are able to connect with potential suppliers, contractors, and marketing people throughout the world. If you are going to sell directly into the Chinese market, for example, you must, by law, have a Chinese citizen as a partner in your firm.

It may be that your partnership might extend to only one of several business ventures or activities with which you are connected. It could also be that this partnership is mutually agreed to be only a temporary arrangement that will be dissolved when your venture is sold. Alternatively, one partner may have a pre-arranged agreement to buy out the other once one of the members reaches a certain age or the company obtains a given level of sales.

Corporations

Incorporating your company offers tax advantages, but also a number of responsibilities, such as having a board of directors, annual meetings, shareholders, designated company officers, and financial reporting deadlines that must be met.

While your company may ultimately become a Corporation, for most small businesses the Limited Liability Company, LLC, is a much more convenient way to go. There are many fewer filings, and your LLC can be a solely owned company or a partnership. You can also change your company's status, location, or ownership with an LLC much easier than with a corporation.

Filing your documents for an LLC will be covered in Chapter 9. In general you will need to consult with an attorney and likely an accountant to make sure you are in compliance with present laws.

Non-Profits

If you have a passion for helping others by sharing the information that you have learned through your life experiences, founding a non-profit organization would be a logical path to follow.

A typical model is the TV preacher who started off with a single congregation, built up to a mega-church, now has a TV show, and is part of a Bible College where his ministry is being taught to those who may have followed his career since they were children. The late Billy Graham is a recent example.

Evangelism in the meaning of spreading The Gospel may not be your thing, but you must evangelize your message with a similar passion and commitment. Often this message uses some religious concepts. These might include love of humanity, offering hope to those in crisis, and helping the afflicted to see their afflictions as things than can be overcome. They may be challenges that can be turned into mentally and financially profitable undertakings, rather than a road to despair, depression, and ruin.

To be reasonably undertaken, a non-profit organization needs to have a series of declared purposes and a mission that sets it apart from other such organizations. If your goal is in the general category of "helping your fellow man," perhaps going to divinity school and becoming an ordained minister is the path for you to take.

A non-profit organization needs to be narrowly focused with a clearly defined objective. Your non-profit might be to help eliminate some disease that impacts millions that is largely unknown. Closer to home, you might want to assist the homeless in finding winter shelter in your home county. Or maybe you want to help raise money to finance learning opportunities for underserved populations within your state or country.

Whatever this desire is, it needs to be followed by a clear plan of action that outlines:

• Who you are and the qualifications of your board of directors?

• What are the objectives of the non-profit organization.?

• How your organization fits with other community non-profits including areas of potential cooperation and conflict.

• How the money to fund the organization is to be raised, and if any corporate sponsors are already committed.

• A budget that shows operating costs including when and how money is to be dispersed.

• What are the racial, sexual, and financial demographics of the community that you hope to serve?

- Tracking measures for judging the success of your program.
- Periodic public reports to funders.
- Audit procedures.

To support your case for starting another non-profit that competes for the same pot of money as other service organizations in your community, it is necessary to prepared the ground by having members of the community and the heads of local non-profits testify that your efforts can provide a practical means of helping to solve a real community problem.

Is all of this necessary for every effort that results in a non-profit company? Truthfully the answer is no. However, it would be a very fruitful exercise to plan for the day that you must testify before your Secretary of State who might challenge your unlicensed non-profit as a fraudulent activity designed to extract money from the public for your personal use.

As soon as you have advanced sufficiently, you should also submit materials to organizations that rank non-profits and seek to get your non-profit as a member of national community funds drives. All of this will require that you establish a legal and ethical existence to stay off lists of suspect non-profit organizations.

Chapter 7

Starting Your Business with Minimal Capital

Takes money to make money. You do not need a fortune to get started.

∞ ∞ ∞

Getting start-up money is always a challenge and frequently requires personal sacrifice. If you have stashed some money away over previous decades you are in reasonable shape. You may not have enough in your personal savings to do everything you want right away, but at least you have something to use for your initial business filings, product development, etc.

In Chapter 4, I discussed how your short-term business might raise capital by using eBay as a means of raising immediate money for living expenses.

Hopefully after you were laid off you received a settlement for past service, and a portion of this money might be used to finance your new business venture and help keep your family afloat. I like my "Rule of Thirds" here.

If you received a cash settlement package, reserve one third of that amount to live on, one third to start your business, and the remainder to take care of those unanticipated expenses, such as those that might be caused by accident or illness.

After you have firmly selected your business, how much more money do you need? If you have whole life insurance policies you can often borrow from them at lower rates than you can get from banks. These rates are often set at about 5%, depending on what the interest rates were at the time that the policy was started.

Things Not to Do

It is tempting to use your credit cards to get some fast money to start your business, but however tempting and easy it might be to use them, do not get yourself into a sustained debt situation with these cards. They are fine for covering travel expenses, etc., provided they are paid off immediately. However, once you start running a balance of the thousands of dollars, interest rates quickly build the total balance to the point where you cannot earn enough from your nascent business to pay them off.

It is better to defray, reduce or postpone an activity rather than create a revolving debt crisis with credit cards that you cannot realistically discharge before you get your business off the ground.

There are few businesses indeed where quick profits in the range of 20 to 25 percent can be anticipated. If you find yourself in this situation, you can sometimes get a short-term reprieve by transferring debt from one card to another. You will still owe the debt, but you may carry a balance at no interest for a few months. Several such activities will reduce your credit rating.

The only activity that is worse than credit-card debt to finance your business is pay-day lending where even higher interest rates and penalties are assessed. Stay away from this one too.

Alternative Business Plans

You have chosen the thing you want to do, now is the time to concentrate on the how you are going to do it with the resources that you have. Even if you had the resources, it would be foolish to start breaking ground on a large production facility until you could demonstrate that you had a market to serve.

Your initial business plan should have as its objective the proof of concept. Is whatever you plan to do possible, and how do you demonstrate that possibility to yourself, potential investors, and banks?

Ideas are worthless unless they can be demonstrated. This demonstration may take the form of a prototype product. It might be a case study. It could be a book outline, sample chapters, and a completion date. Perhaps you have a movie script in progress that needs to be finished. Something tangible must be produced. What is the least costly physical plant that you can think of to make that physical or intellectual product?

Maybe this can be done in a rented space where

tools and administrative services are shared with other entrepreneurs. A number of universities and regional developmental organizations have such spaces for the temporary use of developers.

Perhaps you need to go off and hibernate somewhere to work on your project for three months. Writers' colonies have been established for just this purpose. While you will have periodic contact with your fellow writers, most of the time spent in such places is in solitude at your computer. Spaces are usually awarded by application and nothing works better than to be personally introduced to members of the governing board of the organization.

While the ultimate vision of your product or service may be world-wide, this initial approach must be scaled down until you have a method of starting your project that you can financially undertake.

Go online and look for case studies of how successful people developed their prototype ideas. Even though they are likely working in different fields, whatever methods that they used might be adaptable to your situation and allow you to direct your limited resources to things that are proven to work.

It never hurts to ask any successful business person, "How did you get started?" If you are in a situation where you can discuss business concepts, such as at a conference or trade show, some very valuable insights can be obtained. Everyone had to start somewhere, and most of these starts were small-scale operations which were enlarged as their businesses grew.

Raising Start-Up Capital

Asking your relatives to put money into your project is fraught with perils. Your parents have already invested very heavily in your future, and to ask them for even more financial aid is pushy at worst and disingenuous at best. What money they have accumulated is likely going to have to last them for the remainder of their lives. This is not money that the average American family can put at risk.

On the other hand, if they are independently wealthy, regularly donate to political causes; perhaps a little start-up money could be obtained, if you can build a proposal that is good enough to convince them that their investment is sound.

If family members are not willing, or unable, to make a direct investment, perhaps they would purchase some of your products or buy an advance block of tickets for your theatrical pro- https://www.Kickstarter.com duction. Maybe their https://www.gofundme.com support could be in the way of in-kind services where they are lawyers and file your legal paperwork for you.

Backers

Raising capital from individuals or venture capital funds was formerly most commonly done by presenting your concept to a board or financial committee. The popular business TV series "Shark Tank" is an example of one way such meetings might be conducted, although restructured as an entertainment platform. These are loans that must be repaid and/or may be at the costs of the backers having some retained interest in the company.

Making such presentations implies a commitment by you that if your application is accepted that you will go through with the transaction. However, nothing is a contract until it is a contract. Just because you approach one group of venture capitalist does not mean that you cannot approach others at the same time or that you must accept an unfavorable offer.

There are now alternatives, like crowd funding, where you appeal directly to the public at large with your concept in an attempt to raise money for your start-up. Kickstarter and Go Fund Me are two such platforms. They differ in detail, but have raised millions for start- ups over the past decade. This is also a way to test your concept before you become too deeply invested in your business. To cover their operating expenses they will take a percentage of the money you raise. Since this is free money, the amount that they skim off is not significant.

Kickstarter

Among the first of these online capital-raising companies, Kickstarter has a list of criteria that your project must meet. Typically your concept must result in a physical product which could include a piece of performance art, a book, play or consumer item. Financing a non-profit effort, giving support to handle a life-crisis or political activities are off limits; unless the immediate reason for the project is to write a book, etc. that presents the cause you support.

With Kickstarter you established some amount as your money-raising goal. Say you need $5,000 to finish your book. If you receive pledges for $3,456 dollars during the time that your project is live, the effort fails and this money is never collected from your would-be donors. Typically, the person who is seeking the money offers some reward for the pledge with the amount/number of the rewards increasing with the amount of individual pledges.

If your initial Kickstarter effort fails, you can try again with a different approach. It is extremely helpful to present a short YouTube video where you pitch your idea to potential backers.

This platform allows you to communicate with your backers by accepting and offering comments, updating them of the progress of their efforts, discussing personal appearances, offer free concert tickets and thanking them for helping to fund your project. Should your project bring in more money than your goal, you get to keep the excess, minus the percentage that Kickstarter takes for hosting your effort.

If your Kickstarter project fails and you are satisfied that you have made as good an effort as you could manage, then the economic soundness of your entire effort is put into question. Hard as the truth might be, perhaps there is not the market demand for the product that you thought. If this is so, how do you create that market through effective PR? This topic is covered in Chapter 15.

Go Fund Me

Although there are similarities, Go Fund Me differs in that you are able to raise money for causes or even to alleviate personal hardships. Where in Kickstarter you do not receive anything unless the entire amount is raised, with Go Fund Me any amount raised is sent to the person who initiated the appeal.

Some potential donors operate on one platform and not the other while others work on them both. There is no reason why you cannot launch your appeals to both, although I would not do it simultaneously because of the confusion of your having offered different rewards for each platform to be fulfilled at different times.

No matter how you raise money to start your business, the key point is to minimize your financial risks. Your approach may have to be unconventional, but you need to be sufficiently inventive to not only make your product, but also discover how to do it with the smallest investment possible.

Hovey's Knives of China:
A Personal Example

My concept of Hovey's Knives of China started when I was a child https://hoveysknivesofchina.com and became interested in coinage. One of the most interesting of the world's coins is Chinese knife money which was made during the Chinese Bronze Age some 3,000 years ago. This coinage was stylized replicas of cooking cutlery with a ring at the top so that the coins could be strung on a string for easy transport.

Fast forward through the Korean War, Cold War, Vietnam, the opening of China and the United States becoming the world's largest customer of Chinese-made products. At this stage in my life I was in my late 60s and commonly wrote for the Krause knife publications such as their Knife Annual.

When covering the International Blade Show in Atlanta I found an exhibitor who http://bladeshow.com/ was importing artifacts from China's Bronze Age, including their knives. This revived my interest in these objects and the thought that I could use these ancient bronze designs as inspiration to make kitchen cutlery, such as had not been seen for a thousand years.

New concepts in knives are difficult to derive. To make these knives that were not only new to the market, but also useful cutting implements struck me as a sound business concept. First I made wooden and then cut-out aluminum prototypes. I also enlisted the aid of bladesmith Paul Hjort who helped me establish a shop in a portion of a closed-in breezeway that connected my old plantation home with its external kitchen which had now become my office.

The major part of this reconstruction, including the electrical wiring, was contracted out, but I did the painting and built the benches to hold the grinders, buffers, and oven that I needed. Now that I had the designs, I contracted with Atlanta WaterJet to cut blanks from carbon steel saw blades and sheet stainless steels from which to fashion the knives.

The total costs of building my shop, having the knife blanks cut, producing more than 20 different patterns of knives and exhibiting them at the International Blade show was about $50,000, which is less than the cost of a good truck. The pay out from my endeavor is not the income received from the relatively few custom knives that Paul and I could produce, it will come from licensing the designs to others.

This approach allows me to do research and development, or R&D, on my products. I could test the designs, cook with them, judge potential demand, and get feedback from the marketplace for $50,000 compared to the $5,000,000 it might take to establish a factory. By scaling down my concept I was able to launch my business with minimal financial exposure. This is how to start a company if you are going to make a physical object.

Chapter 8

Choosing a Name for Your Business

Your business name has to be
memorable and easy for people to say
and type.

∞   ∞   ∞

U nless you are trying to hide the nature of your business from the authorities, it is useful for your business' name to say what services are being offered and by whom. Your business name should be simple, memorable, and descriptive. In my own case, I used my distinctive middle name, Hovey, described the class of objects that I was making, knives and where I had derived my inspiration, China. The result was that I named my business, Hovey's Knives of China.

Descriptive Product Names

Ford Motor Company, Winchester Repeating Firearms, Buck Knives and Hoover Vacuum Cleaners are well known companies that incorporated the names of their founders with the products that they made.

I might have called my company Smith's Stuff which would have been accurate, but not particularly informative as to what kind of "stuff," I was selling.

This type of naming is particularly valuable if you happen to be blessed with a distinctive short and memorable name. Even short oriental names like Lu or Kim can work in this context, if linked with something related to the culture, like Lu's Woks.

One-Word Names

Some brands have gotten away with using single names such as Caterpillar, the well-known maker of heavy equipment. While memorable and somewhat descriptive of the track-mounted machinery since both crawl across the landscape, this name might also be applied to garbage trucks since caterpillars are unrelenting consumers of vegetation.

In the 1800s elephants were novelties and captured the public's imagination. This gave rise to a very large number of products that incorporated the name, including soaps and gunpowder. To differentiate all of the potential products that might be called Elephant brand this or that, at least one other word was necessary.

Two-Word Names

Butterflies, wasps, and ants, to name a few from the insect world; and lions, tigers, and rhinos have been adapted to naming uses when combined with another word that describes the product.

Not that we don't have enough insects, animals,

and plants to borrow names from; there are also mythical creatures such as the unicorn which has been linked with countless products. Rocks are also sometimes useful as is the case with Lava Soap, which uses ground pumice to help abrade and scrape heavy greases from the skin.

In the natural food movement, the use of the word farm is very useful as is dairy and vineyard. When these descriptive nouns are combined with the owner's name or maybe even the location, the result may be a useful name. Similarly, the product, like cheese, wine, or barrels might also be made part of a company's name.

Geography has also gotten into the act. Many companies found it convenient to use the name of their home town to brand their products, such as Utica Cutlery, after the historic manufacturing town in New York State. Or you might have Shasta Beer, after Mt. Shasta in Washington State. While not particularly descriptive, such names have come into common use.

Two-word names might include both names of the company's principals or founders, such as Smith & Wesson or Rodgers & Lawrence. If your company was promoting conflict resolution through the use of your book, Lion & Lamb might be a good name with religious implications. Still it would be useful to add another word to make it Lion & Lamb Publications.

Multi-Word Names

The ridiculous extreme of these are the long series of names often applied to legal partnerships where each of the partners have their name inscribed in gold lettering on the door of the firm. Many a comic has mined this material when he sends is supposed client to a firm like, McCorcal, Hammerstene, Goldfarb, Glavinavitch, Ulmit, Whitefeather, and Stone, to use a made-up example of a firm with multi-cultural members. Imagine writing a check to such a company.

For memorability, the ideal number of words in a firm's name should be no more than four with one of those four being the name of the product or service being provided. If you have a distinctive name, that can provide the first word. The formula then becomes Name, ------------, Product.

So the name might become McCorcal's Natural Produce. Or even shortened to Mac's Natural Produce, as I suspect that in the food distribution trade McCorcal would very quickly be shortened to Mac's, or even Mac's Produce, once the name became established.

Letter Names

Of all the ways to derive a company name, the one I like least are those composed of a string of letters. In the U.S. there are large numbers of pharmacies in the CVS chain. To me this could just as well stand for Central Veterinary Supply instead of the letters standing for Consumer Value Store that the company claims that the letters represent. For a start-up company whose only link to a potential customer might be its name, naming with only letters could be a fatal blow.

Computer Teck

Now that we live in the Computer Age and most of the buying public is using screen devices, it is fashionable to derive a company name by tacking a ".com" onto another word or pair of run-together words. Your company may be Vintagerecords.com, Jass.com, Wordsmithing.com, Copyriting.com, Accounting.com, Music.com, etc. Such a name puts a modern face on your product and hopefully also acts as a direct link to your website.

The challenge is to derive a name that is not already used by someone else as a company or domain name. There are a large number of people who make a business of registering logical domain names with the intent of selling the use of them back to companies whose names have a high degree of recognition. This is the reason that you need to protect your brand's name in different ways.

Chapter 9

Getting Legal

In the world of business, crossed T's and dotted I's are a critical component. Get it done right the first time and you never need worry about it again.

∞ ∞ ∞

There are basic facts that you need to establish before you file for the documents that will enable you to conduct your business. At a minimum you will need to have already decided on:

• The name of your business.

• Who are the owner/owners who are filing the papers.

• The legal address of your business.

• The type of business - single owner, partnership, LLC, or corporation.

• Contact information for the company officers.

• What class of products are you producing.

• A description of those products in a single sentence.

• Your agent or legal representation.

I am not a lawyer, and I am not giving legal advice. I am reporting my experiences after having gone through these processes and writing about what I have learned from them.

Always seek qualified legal advice to make sure that you are, in fact, in compliance with all applicable laws. My experiences are also limited to one state, Georgia, which has a relatively simple set of compliance documents compared to other locations, such as New York City or Boston. It also makes a considerable difference whether you are located within a city's jurisdiction or in a rural area.

Initial State and Federal Filings

One of the most valuable attributes that your firm has is its name. In recognition of this most states require that you register your company with the Secretary of State. It is desirable that you have a distinctive name that is unique to your company as was discussed in Chapter 8. This filing and a simultaneous filing with the Federal Government provides you with tax numbers that you will need for future filings and gives you a degree of legal protection for your name.

The details of these filings vary with each state. One online company **www.Legalzoom.com** specializes in assisting individuals with the paperwork needed to file these documents and will send reminders of any follow-up paperwork that will be necessary during the life of the business.

If there is a significant change such as the business becoming a partnership, rather than a single-owner-operator or a change of officers, these filings will need to be periodically amended to reflect the true nature of the business.

A consideration that needs to be decided on very early in the life of business is who owns what rights to the intellectual and physical property that the business owns? If the business started as a partnership between several people who might be considered co-founders, what portion of the business belongs to each and how is any stock in the firm to be distributed.

If there are to be angel investors, do they receive stock in the new firm? How are dividends to be paid, and who determines what these dividends are to be?

Is there to be an annual meeting of corporate shareholders held by the board of directors, and where is that meeting held? How is the pay of the chief executives of the company to be decided and reviewed? These can be complex issues and will need to be visited as the company grows from your concept into a viable, productive company.

These are but a few of the details that need to be included in the trail of legal documents associated with the firm. Each major change in the company will need to be recorded in a legal fashion to prohibit potentially destructive court actions that might arise during later years.

Health and Safety Concerns

OSHA, the Federal Occupational Health and Safety Act, requires employers to have and maintain a safe working environment for their employees, provide regular safety trainings, have safe storage for hazardous materials, issue protective equipment as needed, and allows employees to file reports of potential safety violations to OSHA without recriminations.

Some industrial processes, like welding, have specific regulations on how these tasks are to be conducted. There are regulations regarding the handling and storages of potentially explosive substances, like the acetylene bottles associated with welding units. There are also regulations concerning working in confined spaces, electrical wiring, plumbing, and disposals of industrial waste.

Environmental concerns are covered under separate regulations such as the Clean Water Act which covers the discharge of industrial waste into the ground or released into streams. The safety of the nation's water supplies, that were ignored in the early part of the 20th Century are now considered significant enough to stop the location of some industrial facilities in locations where the nation's waters may be adversely impacted.

Similarly, discharges into the atmosphere can be restricted be they toxic fumes, greenhouse gasses, Freon, dust, volatile hydrocarbons, mineral fibers, or odors generated during the manufacturing process. Carbon dioxide derived from coal-fired power plants, decomposing organisms, forest fires, and thawing of the permafrost in Arctic regions has become a concern by contributing to global warming and sea level rise.

Sometimes these factors may be advantageous such as relocating an industry on a brownfield site, such as a coal storage yard, that is not particularly hazardous to the environment, but is undesirable for other uses, such as the location of a subdivision.

A municipality may grant special tax or other incentives to encourage businesses to build on former industrial sites to increase their tax revenue, create jobs, and clean up a blighted area. Frequently these sites will already have road and railroad access which can cut transportation costs and might even provide worker transportation through a light-rail network.

Union and Work Rules

Unions grew out of a desire to enhance worker safety, improve living conditions, force employers to pay at an appropriate wage level, and protect against arbitrary firings for capricious reasons. Before the advent of Federal safety regulations, the unions were the worker's most effective voices against the excesses of Golden Age Capitalism when the Robber Barons vertical integration of industries included controlling their workers' every act.

An individual who operates his own business and is its single employee, need not to be too concerned with union labor demands, although he might receive goods and services handled by union labor.

Some areas of the country are more attractive to industries because of their general lack of unionization. This is particularly true of the southern states. Large numbers of industries once located in the north have moved south to take advantage of less expensive labor and generally less expensive operating conditions than in their home state due to a milder climate.

Consequences of Climate Change

It is of no consequence whether you personally believe if climate change is man-made or a natural phenomenon. It is happening as it always has and always will. Only 10,000 years ago we had glaciers in mincontinental North America. The level of the sea was hundreds of feet lower than today. Vast areas of land were dry that are now covered by the ocean.

Only because our lives are so short, do we consider the proposition that today's climate is anything more than a temporary segment of earth's dynamic history.

We are in an interglacial period with general melting of the polar ice and a rise in sea level. This is happening on a world-wide basis. While in Nordic regions there is a general rising of the land because of the rebound caused by the melting of the last ice sheet, elsewhere coastal areas are continuing to be flooded and will flood more often in the future.

If you want a more stable environment for your operation, locate away from the coast to escape not only the potential of being flooded out, but also business interruptions caused by tropical storms running along the coasts.

There are an increasing number of building codes in coastal areas that require structures to be built well above ground level to prevent flooding. This helps with water damage but increases the structure's exposure to the wind.

The passing of a storm on the barrier islands might result in the foundation of a structure surviving, but it is now surrounded by water because that portion of the beach has been washed away as the sand has continued its migration in response to wind and tide driven currents.

That beach property may have been delightful when you paid a premium for your water-front lot, but is not so desirable when under two feet of water. In some jurisdictions, such as Louisiana, you even lose your rights to the land if it is permanently flooded.

Chapter 10

Going to the Bank With A Business Plan

Sometimes you must go to commercial sources for capital. Make your best case and walk out with the cash.

∞   ∞   ∞

Now that you have done the preliminary steps to make your product and start your new business, you are likely going to need more money to produce products for your first large-volume sale. You are going to need a loan, and your local bank may be your best way to get it.

What Banks Do

To approach a bank you are likely going to be asked for a series of documents. These include:

1) Personal identification.

2) State business registration.

3) Federal business registration.

4) Information on company officers including legal representation.

5) Records of past sales.

6) Tax filings for past two years.

7) Your business plan.

8) Purchase order for a significant number of products.

Everything seems to be going well until you get to numbers 5 and 6. Fact is you may have sold little or nothing from your shop where you built your prototypes. If you are caught unawares with this demand this usually results in a very long pause. Now you need to produce your business plan to show that you have done your due diligence. This includes a thorough examination of your production and distribution methods, having accurately determined the production costs of your products, and the amount of profit that you project will be realized from the sale.

This is not the bank's money that they are risking, these are the deposits of every school teacher, worker, and retiree in the community whose personal welfare the bank must take into account before they grant your loan. Friendships and past relationships do mean something, but the bank needs hard numbers and reasonable projections that can be independently audited and found to be a risk-worthy venture.

Failures to property vet loans can lead not only to bank failures, but to criminal prosecutions of the bank's officers. Although the largest banks in the nation managed to shelter their officers against prosecution during the credit crisis resulting from the collapse of the housing bubble of the 1990s, this protection does not extend to operators of home-town banks.

Producing a Business Plan

You can cookie-cut a business plan from any number of online resources or books. There are about 50 business plan books on the market at any given time. Some are for specific industries, like movie making, while others are large industries with established track records of sales, market research etc., and fewer are for small guys attempting to start their own business. This plan is going to need to have numbers, prices, customers, and competitors along with a reasonable analysis of market conditions and risks.

Getting your Facts

Having the maximum number of facts at your fingertips often comes at income-tax time. Once these tax documents have been filed, it is time to dive even deeper into costs for each of the products that you produce for each method that you use to make them. By this time you should have arrived at the most efficient way to produce your products or having them made for you.

Each product needs to have a separate analysis. This will ultimately be reduced to a single line of text in a chart or a dot on a graph, but must be firmly and realistically established either by quotes from your producer or actual determined costs for products you make yourself.

A new business is also going to need an understanding of the total market sales for this class of object. There are trade organizations for every industry that spend considerable resources in determining sales, market shares, what segments of the market are increasing, which are in decline, etc. This information will also reveal who your potential collaborators might be, who your competitors are and provide you with the information you need to differentiate your products from the competition.

What are your strong points? Are they in design, price competitiveness, new manufacturing methods, marketing, or selling methods? Making good products turns into a liability if the result is a warehouse of excellently made products that you cannot sell.

How are you going to decide how many of what products you are going to make and sell at what price? It is always dangerous to compete on price alone. Someone, somewhere in the world will undercut whatever price you set.

What does your potential sales force look like. Are they going to be company employees, paid on commission, independent contractors, work telephone banks, or located in India? How many salesmen are you going to need to market the volume of products that you need to sell in order to make your company profitable?

If you decide that you are going to produce the products in your factory, what is the cost of the building, equipment, construction, and legal fees. Factories are not built or permitted instantly. Unless you have a very simple product, it is unlikely that you could fill an order for 1,000 of anything in a single year's time with a built-from-the-ground-up factory. If you can't build it, how are you going to fulfill your contract?

It is perilous to not meet your first delivery deadline, because why would you expect your customer to place future orders if they cannot get their orders filled? It is better to delay an order at the outset to give yourself sufficient time to deliver on your promises. Being forced to be realistic about order fulfillment is one of the real values of writing a business plan.

Those who offer services and intellectual content, like life consultants and authors, also have difficulties in calculating costs and returns even though they are not usually burdened with building a plant. They need to reasonably estimate what their client base is, how it is expected to grow over time, and what means they will use to help insure this growth.

If you write books, for example, what titles have you produced and how have they sold? Did the market you were after give you significant returns? How and why is this book going to do any better? Hope is an insufficient answer in a business plan. Just because the book is well written and meticulously edited does not mean that it will succeed.

When and How Long

The appropriate time to write a business plan is before you need it. The average entrepreneur is awash with excitement dealing with the tangible aspects of starting his new business. Designing products, testing them, talking to potential customers and almost anything else is more exciting than writing a business plan.

Nonetheless, there is an old saying, "A business without a plan is a business planning to fail." If you absolutely cannot bring yourself to do it, find someone who can. That someone may be closer to home than you think, like your school-teacher spouse. You may have married that person because they were different. Now is the time to take advantage of that difference.

Even for a small business, it is not unusual for a business plan to take a month to whip into shape. This is likely to be the longest document than an individual has ever written, and the most complex. This is a daunting task, but like all such tasks it can be broken down into manageable steps. Plans are usually divided into steps like book chapters.

Sections of a Business Plan

Business plans can be as short as a single page or as

long as a hundred pages. The objective is to give as complete a picture of your company and its intended operations and profit potential in as succinct a document as possible.

If one of the sections listed below is only a half-page, give it a title and make it a separate page and leave the remainder of the page white. That way someone who is interested in that section can find it easily and fax or send it to a separate reviewer without disclosing other information. If a section is only a line or two, then combine these on a single page.

Rather than being one huge bound document it is better to have the plan in a three-ring binder with tab separations if this is something that is going to run over 20 pages or so. Even allowing for generous portions of white spaces, a small start-up business should be able to keep its business plan to that length.

• Executive summary. This provides a brief overview of the purpose of the business, how the product is produced, and what is its potential market. As an exercise, you should be able to condense this down to a single sentence. You want to be able to concisely answer, what does your business do?

• Product or service. Now in more detail describe the nature of your product or products, including the how and where they are to be made.

• Where you are. At what stage of development is

your business at this time? Hopefully, you are beyond the concept stage and have something tangible in the way of a screenplay, book, or prototype product to present to potential investors.

• Define your market. Be as specific as possible as to the demographics of your potential customers, the potential size of the market, their location, and buying habits.

• Selling to your market. This can be as simple as a list of potential selling tools like through eBay, a Facebook site, webpage, local merchants, YouTube, ads in trade magazines, attending trade shows, appearances on radio shows, TV, newspaper ads, door-to-door solicitations, demonstrations, etc.

• Income. How are you going to make money with your business? What levels of revenue appear to be achievable? Seasonal promotions and sales can play a part in some markets. You should be able to project an annual profit margin, and be able to compare this to previous year's performances.

• Debts, salaries and payments. These are measures of the expected cash expenditures of your company. These should be divided into fixed expenditures like rent, variable expenditures like your power bill, labor costs, shipping, advertising, transportation etc.

Without hard information it is likely that you will overestimate your income and severely underestimate your expenses on your first attempts at a business plan. A more accurate estimate may be made after the business has been operating for a few years.

• Product cost. With data derived from the previous section the real costs of your product or services can be derived.

• Competitors. Is your likely competition likely to be local, national or international? Who are they? What part of the market share do they control? How does your product differ from that offered by your competition?

• Legal considerations. Is your product protected by copyright, patent or by some other means? If so, how much longer do you have patent protection?

• Wants. Often the reason for preparing a business plan is to obtain a loan to finance some expansion of your business. This is far from the only reason to do a plan, but is likely the most common.

You must be able to clearly define what you want, whether it is a sum of money, a partnership, or trade arrangement. You must also make the decision if you are willing to give up part ownership in the company to secure it.

Of all the stages of a business plan this is often either omitted or left unclear. Do your research first, and ask for what you need to have to insure that you can accomplish your objective. To have to go back in mid-project for additional funds does not speak well of you and would causes investors to wonder if they backed the right horse.

At The Bank

However informal you might be at work, you want to be well scrubbed and well-turned-out when you go to the bank. Your objective is to arrive with everything that you need to present your business plan and not have to make return trips. You should have called to make sure that a Loan Officer would be available to see you and make an appointment.

Presenting a business plan in the bank is something like performance art. Usually you are sitting across a table that is large enough for the loan officer to spread out your materials.

After the introductions, you state why you came to the bank and give him your business plan. You will want to know the amount of money that you need. If that amount is too large for the officer to approve, he will send you to someone else who can approve a higher-value loan.

You want to be relaxed, sharp, and informative. If you are a morning person, schedule your appointment for early in the day. If you are more of a night person then the meeting can be much later or even after business hours. Most often this meeting will be during normal business hours in a bank.

As a courtesy the Loan Officer may offer you some coffee, tea or water. It is prudent to refuse it. It is very easy with the distractions of the meeting or your excitement about making a point that you could easily knock a water bottle or spill coffee over the table and your documents.

A little visible apprehension about your meeting is expected, but stay as calm as possible. Either write down or record what was said. Usually your loan will not be granted on the spot. Your banker will take it up with the bank's loan committee; they will do a credit check, look for criminal convictions, and take action on your loan.

At some later date you will receive notifications that the documents are ready, and you can go to the bank's attorney's office and sign them. Now that you have the bank's money, you had best be ready to make and sell some products.

Chapter 11

Protecting Your Brand

You have a business. Now you must make sure someone else cannot legally take it away from you.

∞ ∞ ∞

T he U.S. Patent and Trademark Office and the Copyright Office have https://www.uspto.gov/ upgraded their requirements to allow for patents, trademarks, and copyrights to be applied for online and offers a reduced price if all of the filings and review processes can be conducted electronically, although the system is slow and clunky.

While it is desirable for trademarks and copyrights to be applied for by individuals, patents are most often written by registered Patent Attorneys who work closely with the inventor to insure that the complex patent requirements are submitted in the proper manner.

Differences Between Patents, Trademarks and Copyrights

Of these three categories of intellectual property, patents are the most involved, difficult to obtain and take the longest time to be granted. Patents are meant to protect inventions for a period of 20 years so that the inventor retains the exclusive rights to his invention for that period.

Trademarks are elements of design which represent the company or individual that is linked to the company's brand. A trademark may be applied to all garments made by a clothing company even though they might include shirts, trousers, and underwear.

Copyrights are applied to works of authorship which might include books, poems, songs, music, plays, screenplays, movies, photographs, paintings, software, and sculptures created by a writer, artist, or programmer.

It may be that all three might be linked to the same product, but they each must be applied for separately. For example, a design of cookware might be protected by a patent, carry the company's trademark, and its use described in a copyrighted cookbook.

Trademarks

One of the earliest things that should be done in business development is to design and register your trademark. This is a reasonably simple process although it must be done with excruciating exactitude. Your trademark may incorporate numbers, words, colors, and graphic designs.

Once these are settled on a drawing is made and submitted to the U.S. Patent and Trademark Office and the process started. When you arrive at the website you are given choices as to what action you wish to take.

The U.S. Patent and Trademark office has several simple tools to help you understand what a trademark is and how to properly make your application. There is a short video overview, a longer 40-minute version, and a 36-page booklet, Protecting Your Trademark: Enhancing Your Rights Through Federal Registration, which are all available from www.uspto.gov.

Why You Should Have a Trademark

Trademarks are the means by which consumers identify your products, separate them from unlicensed copies, and provide instantly recognizable branding. This is particularly valuable for consumer goods, but is also valuable for books and other things that you might publish.

In my own case my business books are published under the **PROFIT**® brand, which is my U.S. registered trademark. While you may not trademark a word, as I have apparently done here, you can trademark a word that is rendered in a particular type font or enclosed in a particular device, such as an oval, star, rectangle or other shape.

Trademarks, of themselves, may have value. President Trump, for example, has made millions on licensing the use of his name on hotels, golf courses, casinos, etc. In this sense, if you have a common or uncommon name, does not mean that you have the rights to use it to trademark your business, if someone else has already registered the name.

In selecting a trademark design that will be allowed by the USPTO, it needs to be distinctively recognizable, able to be defended against potential infringers, and is stronger if it does not contain the names of commonly used products or services. Smith's Baked Goods, for example, would very likely run into instant conflict with many other Smiths who happen to also bake and use their name or their products.

Similarly, geographic names are also confusing such as New York --------, almost anything. Often these would not be allowed for formal registration even though this might be the name over your shop. It is better to use a name for your bakery to be some made-up word like "Breadworks on 42on," if it happened to be in New York.

It is not legally required that you register your trademark, but you gain significant protection if you do. The U.S. government will not defend your trademark. If there is an infringement, you must defend your rights. The staff in the trademark office will assist you in completing your application, but cannot offer legal advice. For legal consultations you need to engage an attorney who specializes in the protection of intellectual property rights.

How to Apply for a Trademark

Say that you have some ideas about your proposed trademark. The first thing you must do is search to see if anyone else has already used your mark or something so similar that your mark would be an infringement. This is done on the "TESS search trademark system." You are required to do this search as part of the application process.

You can file your application for the least costs at the Trademark Electronic Application System (TEAS) at http://www.uspto.gov/teas. There are several options on exactly how to file and how to pay. Generally the more work you are willing to do to complete your filing online, the less your application will cost.

On your application, you will be required to produce a written description of the mark and also supply a drawing. The drawing is generally rendered in black and white, unless color is claimed as a distinctive part of the trademark. In submitting a drawing, a "standard" character drawing allows the use of different fonts, letters that are in the trademark database. "Special Form" drawings are required if there is a special design, logo, or color associated with the trademark.

On your application you must also lists the goods and/or services that you are claiming under your mark. These may be something like woodworking supplies and woodworking craft instruction. These must be identified with an ID manual as to the exact class of goods being trademarked. This aids the electronic search process.

In filing your application you will be asked to state when the trademark was first used and to submit a sample of your trademark on a document to prove that the trademark has been used in commerce. This may be in the form of a shipping label or tags on clothes. This is a less expensive filing that one done under the "intent to use" category. This sample is identified as a "specimen" in the documents. Things not allowed as specimens are invoices, announcements, PR materials, letterhead and business cards.

After you file you are required to check the status of your application. It is not uncommon for a first application to be rejected. If these objections can be overcome by sending in new materials or otherwise supplying additional or corrected information, the application will be allowed to proceed.

You will be assigned an examining attorney who will work with you for the completion of your application, once all parts of it are in acceptable condition. This is usually about three months after the application was submitted.

After all objections have been overcome and all fees paid, the attorney will release your application for publication in the Trademark Official Gazette, and you will receive notification of publication. If there is no opposition to your application, the Trademark will be granted and you will receive an official certificate from the Trademark office.

You will also receive numerous unsolicited offers to register your trademark in foreign countries, for legal representation, and for many other presumed needs. These are not sanctioned by the USPTO, and most are spam. If you decide to use the services of some of these firms, research them thoroughly first. In many cases their efforts results in high costs, but few real benefits to your company.

At the end of 6-year and 10-year periods the owner must file a Declaration of Use to continue his Trademark protection. There is a six-months grace period, but following that you must reapply to keep your trademark in force.

Using Your Trademark

Before you receive your trademark you may use the letters TM above your proposed trademark for goods and SM for services which signifies that you intend to use this name or device. You may use these designations whether you intend to register the trademark or not.

After your trademark is granted you are allowed to use the R within a circle designation, PROFIT®, to indicate that this is your U.S. registered trademark and is protected under U.S. law.

Payment

The Trademark Office uses a sliding-fee scale with charges relating to how the mark was described, what actions the department found necessary to process the application, the size of your business, and if you completed the entire process through an electronic filing.

Currently these charges range from between $225 for the all-electronic filing of a simple trademark to $400 or even higher if the trademark covers several classes of goods or services or requires a lot of reworking. The five-year Affidavit of Use fee is currently $125 and the 10-year Affidavit, $425 per class.

These fees will increase to make the department more nearly self-supporting. Although once all fees are paid and the trademark is granted, there are no additional annual fees. As of 2017, the Trademark office no longer accepted cash. You can see their current fees at: http://www.uspto.gov./trademarks/tm_fee_info.jsp.

Copyrights

As was the case of trademarks, the creator of a written document or piece of art is automatically granted the rights to use it under U.S. copyright law. This protection extends not only to exact copies but also to derivative works. In the music industry these rights often give rise to conflicts since many elements of songs and someone else's past performance may be inadvertently incorporated into the new composition.

Musical compositions may come to the mind complete with words, music, and how the piece should be performed. Your subconscious drawn on all your life experiences to make this in the theater of the mind, and because it is drawing on what you have experienced, rips from other people's materials may be included.

A similar process goes on in any creator's brain. In recognition that few things indeed are altogether new there is the concept of "fair use," where small borrowings and even quotations may be allowed in someone else's copyrighted work, so long as the intent is not to deprive the originator of potential revenues from his work.

If someone writes a gospel tune, and a performer turns these words into a jazz composition, this is a "derivative work." Performance rights need to be secured for the altered tune if the material is protected under copyright law, which usually extends for 70 years after the death of the creator.

Why You Should Copyright Your Material

The owners of a piece of copyrighted material have significant legal protections. To quote from Copyright

Basics published by the U.S. Patent and Trademark Office:

Registration establishes a public record of a copyright claim. Registration is necessary before an infringement suit may be filed in court (for works of U.S. origin).

If made before or within 5 years of publication, registration establishes prima facie evidence in court of the validity of the copyright and of the facts stated in the certificate.

If registration is made within 3 months after publication of the work or prior to an infringement of the work, statutory damages and attorney's fees will be available to the copyright owner in court actions. Otherwise, only an award of actual damages and profits is available to the copyright owner.

Registration allows the owner of the copyright to record the registration with the U.S. Customs Service for protection against the importation of infringing copies.

In my own case one of my books Backyard Deer Hunting was being unlawfully reproduced in England and given away as a promotional incentive to join a commercial website. This would have been no problem had they either: A. bought the books on the open market, then they could do anything they liked with them, or B. licensed the rights to produce the books from me.

As they had done neither, I sent a letter complaining of their activities and they stopped the illegal distribution of my books.

Even though it would have been possible to seek damages from the parties, the small amount of money that might have been returned would be more than offset by the legal fees I would have incurred to solve this problem.

The U.S. government will not bring lawsuits on behalf of a copyright owner for potential infringements. The prosecution and costs of all trademark, copyright, and patent lawsuits must be paid by the owner.

How to File for Your Copyright

Although the U.S. Patent and Trademark Office publishes materials about copyrights, the filing of a copyright is done through the U.S. Copyright Office which is a department of the U.S. Library of Congress. Their general website is: www.copyright.gov.

The fastest way to file for a copyright is to use the electronic copyright function which is rendered as "eCO." A word of warning is that this is an old, clunky electronic system. It is very slow and downloads take so much time to complete that you may think that your computer is frozen.

Stay calm. Let those slow government electrons get their acts together and form up on your screen. In order to successfully download the forms, you will need to turn off your pop-up blockers and set your computer's security system on medium. If you do not, you cannot complete the forms.

The first thing I would do is go to the eCO Help Desk. To get there go to:

https://www.copyright.gov/eco/help/ . You will find sections titled, "Registering a Claim in eCO, Uploading Electronic Files in eCO, Submitting Hard Copies of Works (to the Library of Congress), Paying Fees in eCO, Privacy and Troubleshooting."

The methods are reasonably complete and well described, but the slowness of the system and completing the detailed requirements will try your patience. It is also annoying that you will be periodically "timed out" while you are working on your forms, that downloads of book-length manuscripts are very slow, and the sizes of the files are restricted.

For a 200-page book, it is usually necessary to make two downloads. In addition, you will often need to send physical copies of books, musical CDs, and other representations of your materials to the Library of Congress.

Faced with the fluster of getting this done, many originators contract out this service either through their publisher or some independent online resource. Be very careful who you use. You may discover that the person who administers your filing may steal your copyright and file it under his own name or have you unknowingly agree to some restrictions to your copyright.

In short, they may want a piece of the action. The U.S. Government will offer no help here. You can file a complaint against the service that you used with the Copyright Office, but it is up to you to defend your rights in court.

Where and How to Show Your Copyright

Books have a copyright page that immediately follows the title page in the book. There your copyright is stated by making the copyright symbol ©, your name, a comma and the year as in, © Wm. Hovey Smith, 2018. This designates that you are claiming exclusive rights to the book, play, music, etc. that you have published.

There are some things that cannot be copyrighted. These include recipes. You may write and produce a cookbook and copyright that book, but you cannot copyright a recipe. If you have a recipe you can protect that as a "Trade Secret" and keep it secret. If you publish it on a blog, newspaper, on the radio, etc., it then falls into the "Public Domain" and anyone may use it or even reprint it in their own book.

Domains

In the e-commerce era the more common use of the word domain is the protection of your website, blogs and Facebook pages which will be discussed more fully in Chapter 15. Unlike patents, trademarks, and copyrights, these names are sold by private companies who register them in a universal database. An individual may register any number of domains.

Often a person who has the expectation of launching a brand will register several related domains to prevent others using say a .co instead of a .com from pirating his potential customers.

The use and registration of domains combined with patents, trademarks, and copyrights constitute a part of a company's intellectual property which may be as valuable, or more valuable, that the hard assets owned by the company.

Chapter 12

Getting a U.S. Patent for Your Invention

Put the weight of the federal government's full protection behind your invention to keep someone from stealing it.

∞   ∞   ∞

A U.S. Patent is the strongest protection that U.S. citizens can have to protect their creations. However, not everything can be patented. What I learned from working patents for an international company is being applied to the following section.

I am not a lawyer and do not presume to give legal advice. In the discussion of copyright, trademarks and domain names it is entirely possible, if a hair-pulling process, for inventors to file for these protections themselves. With patents it is a necessity to work through a licensed patent attorney to attain a patent that will pass the review process and be granted.

Presently the U.S. Patent Office has a serious backlog of patent applications, and it may take several years before a patent is granted. In the meantime the product may be protected by a "Patent Pending" notice on the product, and this will enable your product to be sold while your patent application is in progress.

A danger is that if you release your product before

the patent application process reaches the patent office, it will not be allowed. It will be in the public domain and may be made by anyone.

Types of U.S. Patents

There are three types of patents that may be granted. These are:

Utility patents which cover new products and manufacturing processes.

Design patents that enable an originator to patent a new design of an existing product. For example, if you render a different design of potato peeler with a futuristic handle featuring an action hero, you could patent the ownership of that particular design.

Plant patents do not relate to industrial plants. These patents refer to biological organisms that have their DNA altered through selective breeding or biological gene insertion to make a variation of a plant with improved characteristics, such as resistance to diseases or increase its drought tolerance.

What Can't be Patented

• If your product is described in a printed publication, in public use, exhibited at a trade show or otherwise available to the public prior to the claimed date of invention.

• If your product has been previously filed by another inventor.

• If your product is a concept or idea that has yet to be built or demonstrated.

Unlike copyrights where the created object is protected as soon as it is completed, patents are not. Inventors must take great care to insure that what they have made is not described in print in anything that could be seen by the public, shown on a YouTube video, or told about on a radio show. Any of these events can cause the product to be disallowed for patent protection.

The objects can be described in private communications which are protected and information circulated to potential backers, but the details of the product may not be revealed. For example, you may be working on a new electric car. Many of the features used in this car may be patentable.

While you might release information about the car in general, you should not describe the details of the new feature that you want to protect by patent – say a new method of breaking a vehicle. You could perhaps say that your vehicle has an advanced braking system, but not describe how it works.

As to point 2, part of the patent application process is to attempt to discover all prior patents in the U.S. and international patents that cover what you are patenting and explain in detail how your product is significantly different. This difference must be of a substantial nature. Changing the color or lengthening a component, like a gun barrel, does not make that firearm a new product.

Ideas and concepts are not, of themselves, patentable; but if this idea is for a new method of making something, say 3-D printing of a certain automobile component, that may be patentable, as a method of making that and similar objects. However, that potentially patentable method may be already be covered by one of the claims filed with the 3-D printer you are using or under a competitors' claim. This is why a very thorough search of the world's patent literature is necessary.

The U.S. Patent office has its more modern patents on a computer-searchable database. Patents issued from 1790 to 2000 are on microfilm. In practicality, the way this works in industry is that over the decades industries have accumulated paper copies of significant patent documents in their files.

One task I did as Information Scientist was to put abstracts of companies' product-related patent information into a searchable database. This way anyone using the search program on their word-processing software could be immediately taken to the appropriate patent; rather than pawing through a dozen file cabinets hoping to run across patents that were related to what he was doing.

What an Inventor Needs to Do

Although the inventor may be working through a patent lawyer, much time and effort will be saved if he writes a mock patent according to the rules and shaves as many hours as possible off his attorney's bill.

Title

Often the first words of the title of a patent are, "A Process, A Device, A Method, A New Configuration of Matter, A Plant, etc. The second part of the title further elaborates on the nature of the claimed invention and often reveals the purpose of the invention which could be, "A Process for Purifying Air."

You might also tell, in a word or two, something of the process and the title becomes, "A Process for Purifying Air Using Bio-Mechanics." This title passes the test of being brief, but does it actually state what the patent is all about? It is on shaky ground because it describes "A Process" which has to be more than a concept.

If the patent is describing a large-scale industrial machine with biological and mechanical components, then the better rendition of a title would be, "A Mechanism for Large-Scale Air Purification by Bio-Mechanical Means" which might be further shortened to: "A Bio-Mechanical Device for Large-Scale Air Purification." This could easily print on the first two lines of a patent document.

If there are other features of the invention that are significant to its operation these could be added so the final title becomes, "A Solar-Powered Bio-Mechanical Device for Air Purification," and drop the "Large-Scale," because market research might reveal that your most viable market is selling smaller units to homeowners, rather than huge units that might be installed on the entire roof of an enclosed mall or factory.

References to Related Patents

This is a listing by patent number of previous patents that relate to the thing that you are patenting. If some of the patents are international or foreign patents, they will be identified by abbreviations associated with their patent numbers.

Statement of Federally Sponsored Research

In most cases no Federal money will have gone into researching a product patent, but if so that contribution will be acknowledged here.

Things invented by Federal employed officials working in their capacity as employees of the Federal Government are considered to be in the public domain. What part of any such work that may be covered by patents and to whom those patents may be assigned is a thorny problem that is sorted out on a case-by-case basis.

In some cases it might be desirable for research to be published in the form of a patent to allow it to be freely and quickly circulated world-wide, with the rights to such a patent being invested in the U.S. Government. Drug research being done by the Centers for Disease Control, like the annual flu vaccine for example, might result in a product that could be patented, but it is considered in the public good not to take that step.

Name

The name of the inventor or inventors is in the next line. In any company it is a boost up the advancement ladder if you are associated with one of the company's patents. This gives you credit with your peers and coworkers. These names are not in alphabetical order, but are listed according to their significance in creating the patent.

Although the individuals' names are on the patent and will appear each time the patent is cited, most typically the patent has been assigned to a company. When referenced a patent might be, Smith, (Patent Number), Date, Title of the Patent. Usually only the first author's name is cited.

Sequence Listing on CDs

If CDs (compact discs) are supplied with the patent containing computer programs or appendices that are referenced in the document, this list tells the number of items on the CD, what this information is, and how it is identified.

Background of the Invention. What is the reason for the invention? How does it compare with what was generally known as "prior art" in that field and how has it improved it? In this discussion you would explain the patents that were referenced at the beginning of the patent with sufficient depth that you can refer to them again in the detailed descriptive section, and explain how your invention offers a novel solution to the problem that these previous efforts failed to solve.

Brief Summary

This describes how your mechanism, device or novel production method operates in general terms.

For example on our theoretical Bio-Mechanical Device for Large Scale Air Purification you might say, "I have made the unexpected discovery that large scale solar-powered devices with rotating trays covered with growing media and colonies of selected mosses and ferns can remove large amounts of particulate air particles and nitrogen oxides from the air to simultaneously purify the air and enrich the growing media." You should be able to describe your invention in one-to-three sentences.

Brief Descriptions of Drawings

A number of drawings are usually included in the application. One shows the entirety of the invention, often showing two views, say from the top and front. Then there may be sections through the invention showing the details of the patentable features and particularly those that are described in the patent claims.

Drawings are usually rendered as clear black and white renditions. The descriptions should be brief, but clearly name the parts of the mechanisms so that they can be easily identified from reading the patent's description.

In preparing the patent materials there is usually an active interchange between the draftsman and the person writing the description. It is desirable that the person writing the process do a sketch, however crude, of what he is describing to assist the draftsman. Drawings are not required, but if the device is at all complex and there are several claims, they will be necessary.

Detailed Description of the Invention

Now that the reader has read all of the proceeding information and has the drawings in hand, the patent writer must describe how the invention works and how his novel invention has sufficiently improved the state of the art as to warrant the granting of a patent. He must lay the groundwork for the following section where he describes his claims.

It is significant that these improvements are non-obvious. If they are considered obvious by the patent examiner, the patent will be rejected; although his decision is often repealed or the obvious sections of the patent are removed and the remainder of the patent re-submitted with fewer claims.

Claims

The claims are listed numerically and described. For example, our theoretical patent application may list as its first claim:

• The use of a solar-powered device to purify air. This would be fine if it were correct that this was a novel invention, but I would strongly suspect that someone else has very likely already patented such an invention.

• A frictionless drive powered by magnetic fields to rotate the plant-containing trays on the roof. The use of magnetic fields to drive mechanisms was well known as early as the 1920s. This claim would likely have to be much more specific to be granted.

• Using rapidly growing mosses and ferns to purify air on a continuous basis. Test results would have to be presented to show that the particular organisms were more efficient than others, like fast-growing grasses, in purifying the air.

• The plant species growing in the media significantly enriched the soil which might be periodically harvested and sold as enhanced plant-growing media.

For the claims to be granted they must be supported by other information in the patent and are often the results of test runs of the invention. Some claims may be dependent on others. A dependent claim will not be granted, if the primary claim is not allowed. The relationships between the claims, the drawings and the descriptions of the patent must be clearly stated.

Abstract

It is often useful to use patent abstracts in many other publications and search-engine applications. In publications where new patents are described these are often printed using exactly the same words as in the patent.

This abstract is, in effect, an advertisement for the patent. It should speak for the patent as if to say, "Here I am, and this is what I do." This message should be as clear as possible to avoid confusion with other patents and uniquely describe the object that is being patented and its novel features.

Conclusions

If you have the impression that the patent application is a complex process with many interrelated parts that must support each other in the application, you are correct.

The lawyer drawing up the patent needs to know enough about the product and its uses that he can reasonably make a case before the examining officials that this is a valid patent and should be granted. Any help, such as the inventor writing up a preliminary document, like a mock patent, will help the process go faster and reduce its costs.

Chapter 13

Locating Your Business

Location is everything, whether in a physical store or cyberspace.

∞ ∞ ∞

Location, location, location" use to be the pat answer to the question, "What is the most important thing to consider when starting a new business?" While that answer is still valid when considering the location of your store-front business, it is not nearly as significant as it once was in this e-commerce society in which nearly all of us participate.

With world-wide connections provided by the internet, a person can manage a multi-million dollar business from his porch in Podunk, Anywhere, with only occasional ventures into the outer world. If you are in the entertainment field or sell services to it, then it makes sense to live in Nashville, New York or Los Angeles. Mercifully, for most of us the best location of our new business venture may be exactly where you are right now.

You may have good cause to relocate to get away from bad weather, exorbitant taxes, pesky neighbors, or any number of other reasons. If you are going to move anyway it would be a good practice to consider if where you are considering going has easy access to high-speed internet, reasonable transportation, and an accessible airline hub when you must make those un-avoidable trips to the world's larger cities.

What is your business, and where would be the optimum location for it? Put another way, does the business location really matter as long as you can easily communicate with the rest of us? If the answer is that it does not matter, you might as well remain where you are and save the relocation costs.

If Richard "Dick" Cabela, his wife and brother Jim can start and run Cabela's, a 3-billion dollar outdoor mail order business, from Sidney, Nebraska, you can do the same, you should feel confident that you can do the same in many other small-town locations in North America. On the other hand, if you are a city creature and cannot think of living anywhere else, then there you should remain.

Favorable Attributes of a Good Location

If you were going to relocate to an new state or country, what factors should determine the location of your new business?

• Accessibility to raw materials. If your raw materials are intellectual, this opens the possibility to locating your business anywhere in the world.

• Ability to ship your products to your customers,

wherever they might be.

• Reasonable taxes and other fixed expenses such as for electricity, water, and sewerage.

• A healthy natural environment. If you are going to spend the remainder of your life there, it is best to select a healthy place.

• Reliable, inexpensive, and safe water supply.

• Don't relocate in areas with known geologic hazards. With the entire country to choose from, don't build on ocean-front property, in an earthquake-prone area, on a flood plain or in an area with frequent fires and/or landslides.

The potential devastation from tornadoes can get you anywhere and hurricanes can sometimes range far inland, but avoid coming geologic catastrophes by locating away from these areas.

• A location that provides access to mental and physical stimulation.

• Reliable health care.

• Accessible emergency services.

• Links to family and friends.

• Pet friendly.

• Productive soils if you plan to have a garden.

• Hunting and fishing opportunities, if these are significant to you.

• Room to build a small structure, if you are going to establish a shop.

• Has reasonable, or no, Homeowner Association rules.

Chapter 14

Running Your Virtual Corporation

To be in business today is to be online. Your customers are looking for you online.

∞ ∞ ∞

Unlike a conventional corporation where there is a fixed location that might manage a business from one place, a virtual corporation might be composed of members from all over the world brought together to solve a particular problem with the understanding that the members will be dispersed after the task is completed.

This is directly analogous to hiring a crew to build a house. Once that job is finished, the crew is dispersed until members are called upon to work on another house. In a virtual corporation there is a crew boss, you, who decides what the task is, contracts with others to do whatever jobs that you cannot do, pays them when that task is done, and continues with your project until you might need to hire someone else to do another part of the work.

As an author putting together a book, I write the first draft of the book and may pay to have it professionally proof read. I will also pay to have it formatted for publication on Amazon and as an e-book. This is comparatively easy for an all-text book. In the past I have also contracted for the printing of the book, but these days I either go with Amazon or a print-on-demand publisher such at Author House.

For an individual, the concept of a virtual corporation is best stated as, "Do what you can and contract out the rest." This way you pay for the services that you need as and when you need them without having to hire employees.

Do It Yourself

The following are a series of tasks that the business owners need to take on themselves.

• Deciding on the name of the company.

• What products or services will be produced?

• What will be the official company address?

• Location of the company's financial resources.

• Making contracts.

• Selecting legal representation.

• Marketing methods.

• Setting project goals and objectives.

• Deciding on buy-out or merger offers.

Contract Out

• Product labor if this is done by someone else.

• Shipping and fulfillment if the volume of shipments becomes so large as to interfere with other aspects of the business.

• Payroll, if any employees are hired on a temporary or permanent basis.

• Tax filings.

• Health insurance, if any is provided.

• Machining and prototype building, if necessary to build your prototypes.

• Manufacturing your product.

The objective of this process is to allow you and your cofounders to concentrate on perfecting the product and building the company, rather than being bogged down with the daily requirements of running a business. It may seem strange to contract out the actual making of your product to someone else.

In today's business environment, it is far better to have someone who has already gone through all the legal challenges of getting his facility permitted than to build your own factory.

A danger in this approach is that you may become so insulated from your potential customers that you lose touch with what they want, what alterations are needed to increase your market share and do not get the chance to see other related business opportunities. To keep this from happening, you should attend appropriate trade shows, take the opportunity to sell your products yourself and maintain a physical contact with your customers.

Some of this contact may be maintained on Social Media as will be considered more fully in Chapter 15.

Chapter 15

Social Media Marketing

Facebook. Twitter. Pinterest. LinkedIn.
May mean nothing to you, but business
moves at the speed of social media
these days

∞ ∞ ∞

There are ever-evolving numbers of online platforms to sell your products or services. Some you manage by yourself, others are developer-managed where you rent space to market your products. Nearly all take a commission from sales and nearly offer training for their members.

Generally you will have an online catalog where you show your products through a series of thumbnails and offer them at a set price or for auction. EBay was one of the first online product-sales outlets. It still has a very large following and remains appropriate for anyone who has a selection of unrelated items for sale.

Amazon, another outlet known to almost everyone, started off as a book buying and selling company, and remains the best outlet for books, far exceeding others like Barnes & Noble in sales. Their Kindle platform is the most popular for e-books, and Kindle books can now be read on any device.

E-Commerce Sites

One way to start is to search for your class of products online and see where others are selling something similar. You may discover, for example, one sales outlet specializes in cosmetic products, although most are more diverse. Others may deal exclusively in firearms or knives while other restrictive E-sales platforms may prohibit such listings. You may not want to be associated with a selling outlet that has many listings for pornographic materials. If you product is more along the lines of personal development or improvement, Kajabi would be an appropriate online outlet. https://newkajabi.com/

BigCommerce offers the opportunity to manage several sales platforms from one site, letting you expose your product to multiple outlets. Shopify is another popular sales outlet that works best once you have established a product line and want to open a virtual store. Both of these platforms offer similar features at similar rates. With BigCommerce you will likely pay slightly more up front and get many premium features included in your costs. https://www.bigcommerce.com https://www.shopify.com Shopify has a less expensive base rate, but adds on costs for advanced features – similar to low-cost airline tickets. These hosted platforms have a monthly rate and you pay a percentage of sales.

If you are a writer you might wish consider publishing through **BookBaby.com**. They will market your e-books to all available platforms, including Amazon. They will take a percentage of the sales price and send you a royalty check when sales reach a threshold value. One recent promotion was that they would publish your e-book on all e-book platforms including those that were yet to be developed. E-books have not consolidated on a standard platform, but very likely will in a few years.

There are also sites that are self-hosting like **WooCommerce** and **Magento**. Both have tools that allow you to custom de-   https://woocommerce.com/
sign your site to encom-   https://magento.com/
pass a variety of product categories. If you sell only one class of products, say T-shirts, one of the hosted sites would probably serve you best and require much less time to put up and maintain.

If your vision has a larger reach, say outdoor camping, where you will have a variety of gear, it would be appropriate to consider a self-managed site. Although not impossible on other sites, sales and other short-term promotions are easiest to manage when you have complete control. A downside is that you will likely have to hire someone to manage the site to extract its full potential.

One good recent overview was done by **Shopify** at: https://ecommerceguide.com

Although they are plugging their own services, they offer good information on other selling sites and links to other company's materials.

Online Product Promotion

If you have strong entrepreneurial instincts, you will have realized that every activity that you do online should interconnect with the products or services that you are offering. The more interconnected your online platforms are, the higher your product will rank on Google search results. As significant as the number of views, you want to use multiple platforms to diversify your market base. Some users go to YouTube first if they want how-to information. This is very much a show-me society. I would advise everyone, regardless of whatever they do, to use YouTube as one of their selling platforms.

Your Website

Websites can be produced professionally or you can use Wordpress or other platforms to design your own. The website can have sev- https://wordpress.org/ eral pages and incorporate YouTube videos. The landing page is where you explain who you are and what you do. Other pages can tell of upcoming events, recent news, list products, post photos and provide contact information for consultations.

If you coach writing and also do business promotion, it would be reasonable to have pages for both.

Websites are also often used as a payment platform using PayPal. If someone wishes to order a book from https://www.Paypal.com my website, for example, they can go to **www.hoveysmith.com** and beneath each book is a PayPal button where they can place the order. You can also put a donation button on your Website page, or feature paid ads for sponsor's products.

Selling products is the best use of a website. If you want to express opinions, blogs are the better vehicles. Facebook pages allow you to do both, but it is better to separate your personal Facebook page from your business page. Those who want to order products do not want to have to page through unrelated materials to find things. If your ordering system requires more than one click to get to the order page, it is too complex.

Facebook

Offering products through Facebook may be done through direct promotions for your own products or through paid ads where you collect a commission on sales through an affiliate arrangement. Once your Facebook profile is sufficiently large, you will receive offers of affiliate arrangements or you may seek them out yourself.

YouTube Videos

You might suppose from the above that I like

YouTube videos. It is not so much that I like YouTube videos, it is that the rest of the world really loves them.

YouTube videos may be used in your Facebook posts to extend the utility of your videos and expand your audience. These dedicated audiences are sometimes referred to as "tribes." This is a useful way of thinking about them because they are composed of those who use your products, offer support, defend against unwarranted criticisms, sign up for your seminars, and go to your events.

From the point of view of the entrepreneur, what other platform allows you to do the following?

• Advertise your product or service at little or no costs.

• Contains exactly the content that you want.

• Can be removed or redone at any time.

• You do not need third-parties to do anything in regards to producing your YouTube.

• So far as we know, stays up forever.

• Actually pays you a little money once you reach a threshold of views.

• Acts as an audition tape for performances, events

like Ted Talks and TV appearances.

It is reasonable to ask, "How do you know?" As of this writing I have two YouTube channels, one for hunting, outdoors and general content, **www.hovey-hunts.com**, and another for my knife company, **www.hoveysknivesofchina.com**.

The Hovey Hunts channel has been up for six years and now has 3.5 million views and 5,000 subscribers. I post on this channel weekly and sometimes more often. The knife channel is just starting and has only a handful of views and fewer than 20 subscribers.

The statistics gathered from your YouTube views do more than satisfy your ego. You can see what content is more often watched, where your dominant market is, what gender your offerings appeal to, and how your channel is gaining views over time. It can also inform you on what percentage of your views are first-time viewers, compared to repeat views from your fans. And yes, you will get fans.

Not everything you put up on YouTube will receive universal acclaim. Your fans will come to your defense against snarky comments. Sometimes you will never know why you might receive a negative content from a viewer.

If you are doing anything worthwhile you will always find those who for good reasons, or sometimes not-so-good reasons, will disagree with you. You need to develop a thick skin about this. Evaluate the criticisms. If they are valid correct them.

My way of doing YouTube videos is to use simple equipment, film, and edit them myself. I am not concerned about minor errors or imperfections. You will do fine on YouTube if you come off as honest, straightforward, and that you are using your experiences to help others solve life's problems. In Chicago and New York, TV quality productions can costs $5,000 or more a broadcast minute. Your costs will be more like $0.50 a minute and maybe even $0.05 a minute, depending on what you are doing and where.

Frequency is important, but don't put up content just because it is Thursday, and the only thing you can think of to say is, "I'm still here." It is logical if you are going to do a complex task to break it down into segments running say 15-minutes each than link three or four of them into 45-minute piece.

One YouTube video can be about your preparations for painting a house. The second video can cover your actually painting your house, and the third video can be about how your house looks after the painting is done. In my case, I might do one on preparing for a hunt, the hunt, and then a concluding one on cleaning and cooking what I killed.

It helps if you can draft someone to stand behind the camera, even if they only make sure you are in the frame and start and stop filming. The cameraman needs to be as economical as possible about what is filmed. The reason is that much of the time spent editing a video is the downloading time. The smaller amount of raw footage and the fewer retakes, the easier the video will be to edit.

Your video needs to be however long is required to illustrate whatever it is that you are doing. In my own videos I try to incorporate something of the unexpected or unusual.

The videos should be honest. If you say you are going to make bear paw soup, that soup is exactly what you should cook. You don't have many words for your title so make them interesting. I have a video, for example, on retrieving cougars in Central Georgia. This happened to be a Mercury Cougar, rather than a mountain lion, although we do have some wandering through the state, and they were historically present.

You may take on something of a persona with your videos. If you do comedy, you can use videos to develop your characters and try them out for your YouTube video before you perform on stage.

You will be able to judge the likes and dislikes and also will receive some comments directly from your viewers. While not quite like the instant feedback from a live event, this information will enable you to perfect your material and presentation.

Once you have your video done, you can set it up so that it automatically posts on your Facebook page, on Pinterest, Twitter and other outlets. This instantly advertises it to other potential views and increases your views.

Pinterest

Pinterest can become an automatic reposting site for photos, YouTube videos, new products, art designs, and anything thing else that can be given a visual presence. On this platform you may have as many "Boards" as you like and page subscribers will receive automatic notifications of any new "pins" that you post.

Each image that you post can be captioned to explain in as much detail as you would like what the significance of this object might be. Authors can put up their new books, artists their new paintings, designers, their latest concepts, inventors their new products, etc.

While tempting to let Pinterest "go on autopilot," it becomes more powerful if your periodically revisit it to add captions and sometimes refresh what you may have said. It would be a good idea to refresh your most commonly posted Boards with new materials monthly.

Should you go on a vacation to Italy you can post your pictures on that site under a heading and add to them several years later when you make a return trip. There is no charge for either the number of channels that you establish or for the numbers of posts.

You also have the ability to modify or remove your pictures anytime you wish. This is an easy site to set up and use and can be used to sell or promote anything that can be expressed in a visual format.

LinkedIn

Although more commonly thought of as a business contact and job search site, LinkedIn can be used for sales and to promote business services. Your appearances, offers to speak on different topics, new books or products may all be introduced on LinkedIn.

This is the best platform to use to contact potential collaborators for joint events, discover those who can offer needed services, and even form your own community around a given product or intellectual concept.

Items like free seminars or trainings may be offered that can be used as a teaser to promote a paid-for event like an on-stage performance, webinar, or subscription newsletter. Newsletters are becoming less popular in favor of more selected product offerings like either call-in or teleseminars.

https://www.lifewire.com/what -is-a-webinar-3486257

The market in general is moving towards events that speak very specifically about a topic, rather than those that have a variety of content. This is true whether you are speaking about a niche product or some self-help or improvement project. Instead of a general, "help improve your life" topic, today's preferred topic would be "quitting smoking" or "overcoming alcohol abuse in families."

As with nearly all modern platforms, LinkedIn can take media in a variety of formats, including written texts, photos, audio segments and my recommenced YouTube videos.

Kickstarter and Go Fund Me

These are but two potential money-raising platforms to both advertise and raise money to start your new business venture. They also act as another means of advertising your products and services to a larger audience.

While these are not selling outlets like eBay, they do accept money and you give "rewards" by way of discounted services or free products at given donation levels. These are discussed in more detail in Chapter 7. As always, these efforts whether successful or not, expose your offerings to a wider audience. They also have the considerable advantage of being able to raise money that does not have to be repaid.

Chapter 16

Local, Regional and International Sales

Act local. Reach global. The entire world is your marketplace.

∞ ∞ ∞

Some businesses are, by their nature, local in scope while others will draw customers from an entire state or region. Ultimately some may reach an international audience. With the potential offered by an interconnected world with the world-wide use of English as the most significant language of commerce, an individual from small-town America can have a world-wide impact. Don't think so? Whoever heard of Bentonville, Arkansas, before Sam Walton started Walmart?

Starting a Local Business

Successful local businesses often offer the following:

• Services within a restricted geographic area within easy reach of their target audience.

• Products that their target customers find desirable that are needed for their every-day lives.

- Routine health or dental care.

- Hair care.

- Educational opportunities.

- Building and home repair.

- Ethnic products for an immigrant population.

- Home living support.

- Utility and water supply.

- Real estate listings and sales.

- Construction equipment sales and rental.

- Sporting activities.

- Hunting and fishing supplies.

- Social activities.

- Religious activities.

- Funeral support.

- Automotive and heating fuel supplies.

- Automotive and farm equipment repair.

- Small engine repair.

- Local fruits and vegetables.

- Home town brewing.

- Loan activities.

- Legal aid.

- Bail bondsman.

- Pharmaceutical and health supplies.

- Antique sales and repair.

- Used household equipment sales and repair.

- Computer repair and troubleshooting.

- Catering and entertainment.

- Florists.

- Crafts, skills and sports teaching.

- Run for a paid political office.

- Life coaching.

- Financial advisor.

- Legal services.

- Security services.

If you want to think about starting something local, run down the lists and see what, if anything, clicks with you. Of those you select, which are you legally qualified to do? Do you have a real estate license, for example? Have you received training as a florist or have you been a small engine tinkerer all of your life? Did you receive some useful training in the military?

Provided that something in this list appeals to you, how many people are doing similar things in your probable service area? Do they offer the same things at even lower prices than you can? Is your market large enough to support another restaurant, for example?

Is your proposed product or services so commonly offered that you are unlikely to get a sufficient number of customers to support you? Should you be a lawyer or plumber, are a sufficient number of people going to need your services to support your practice?

Another possible consideration is how can your proposed business sufficiently differentiate itself to offer something significantly different from your local and online competition? If you find that what you want to do is very similar to what someone else is already doing, perhaps the solution is to propose a partnership or perhaps even an apprenticeship.

New blood and new solutions can sometimes rejuvenate a business that has become too comfortable in its product line and risks losing market share by being replaced by an automated or online competitor.

Local businesses often fail because they offer com-

monly available items that can be conveniently pur-
chased online. Camera stores are now almost completely gone from even medium-sized cities and the
same may be said of the clothing and shoe stores that
use to be in every small town.

The big-box competitors have drained so much of
the communities' cash from potential customer's
pockets that individual store fronts and even malls are
closing throughout North America.

Amazon is well on its way to being able to provide
every American's needs for hard goods, delivered to
their door. Even groceries or pre-made meals are
being ordered online for home delivery. There is even
a danger than these delivery jobs may be replaced by
drones or driverless vehicles.

Regional

Going from local to regional requires interstate
transport of your goods or your willingness to travel
to make speaking engagements or offer services.
Some of these problems can be mitigated by having
others ship your goods or your giving remote trainings
via teleseminars, group telephone calls or supplying
written or video materials. In fact, you might use all
of these methods.

Regionalism implies that whatever you are offering
is somehow restricted to a geographic area. Is that really true? While it is logical to first offer whatever

you have to your local market and slowly expand to regional and international markets, why not try for the world market at the outset? Do not self-restrict your approach to marketing your product.

Types of businesses that are strictly regional in scope and have no international potential are difficult to conceive of in the modern world. Even things that might appeal to a given nationality can sell internationally as populations move around the globe.

Someone from Peru, for example, might find great comfort in finding a local brand of canned food at a Hispanic grocery store in the U.S. Even such a specialized item can have very wide sales. Providing a reminder of home has been capitalized on by generations of immigrants in the U.S. who operate innumerable specialty stores located in major metro areas. A regional approach to tap into this market would be to become a national distributor of specialty foods from South America or South Africa or South Asia.

Things that are bulky and heavy were once restricted to the regions where they were found. This included building stone, sand, gravel, timber and even water. This is no longer true. The same building might have larvikite with blue calcic iridescent feldspars from Norway, marble from Italy, granite from Minnesota with its concrete made from sand dredged from a local river and gravel from a local quarry. A particular type of clean, white sand from my home county in

Georgia is exported all around the nation for use in sand traps on golf courses. The grains are naturally etched and when piled up stand steeper than ordinary river or beach sands.

Approaching a regional market can be useful if your offerings are weather or use specialized, like snow-removal equipment, vehicles suitable for desert transport, crafts designed to be used on large lakes or big rivers, transportation services that move bulk goods or some service that addresses a regional problem – like addiction and depression in sub-Arctic regions. Even so, any of these approaches can have sales and service potentials outside of the areas where they originated.

Foods, like cheese and wine, can have strong regional connections and perhaps may even be branded according to the area that they are produced. Even so, these products now circulate worldwide.

If the metro area is sufficiently large or if your offerings are unique and well-advertised you might draw clients from hundreds of miles, particularly if you engage in online promotions. Your hometown winery or brewery might even be able to capture a part of the national market.

Regionalism can be reinforced by language, legal restrictions, restrictive tariffs, import blocks, or export restrictions. Often political blocks are more significant than the financial ones in restricting trade.

Sometimes political actions on the part of a country will be necessary to clear the importation or export of a class of products. In the case of agricultural items this restriction may be to prevent the spread of a plant diseases. It might also be to protect traditional industries from the stresses of having to compete with inexpensive imports.

The European Market provides subsidies to many small farmers throughout the continent to help them maintain their independent lifestyles instead of having their products replaced by industrial-scale farming.

The same internet tools described in the last chapter can be used to tap into Regional and International Markets. Several services, for example, will insure that your videos will appear in Europe and Asia, as well as in North America.

International Markets

My videos are seen nearly worldwide and my books are available to readers in nearly every country. This is done without me having to ship products to far-away lands or having distribution networks in separate countries. I sell through services like Amazon.com, YouTube and marketing channels that include my videos in their product streams. In exchange I receive additional exposure and revenue that is paid in U.S. dollars.

Such exposures and offers to distribute your products or services are a direct result of your online presence. If you have a blog and only have 100 followers, not much is going to happen. If you have a YouTube channel and have millions of hits and 5,000 followers, then things will happen, and you will start to receive offers for ad payments, product distributions and people asking for your contract services.

For most businesses this amount of exposure is going to take a series of years to accomplish with meaningful inputs added to your content on a regular basis. Reaching an international audience requires even more input, but is entirely achievable.

You have to play the long game by using written, video, TV media and personal appearances. Give presentations at international conferences. Write op-ed pieces for major newspapers. Spend time on the telephone arranging for radio interviews and media appearances. Don't be shy about launching new variations on your product lines to catch market trends.

So what if you don't speak Russian or Chinese? There are a sufficient number of English speakers in those countries to aid you to accomplish whatever it is you need to do.

The common language of most international conferences is English and even if not, simultaneous translations of what you say will be available. Your words may even be available in transcribed foreign-language versions within weeks of the event.

The only thing that prevents many people from having their product make an impact on the international market is that they perceive that they cannot. They think that doing things internationally are too complex, risky and time consuming to accomplish.

Critical things are to get your money up front, make sure the shipping arrangements are correct, that you do not lose any rights from the transfer of property, work through brokers that can handle any necessary customs obligations etc., and that all import fees are paid for by the buyer.

If you are offering services, rather than products, that is usually a more straight-forward business. Usually consultations are billed on a day-rate or contract price plus expenses. The plus-expenses item is important because foreigners are often booked in very expensive hotels in order for the host country to make a good appearance, but room costs of hundreds of dollars a day can quickly consume any profit that might have resulted from the trip.

The same can be said of transportation costs to give a presentation at some Central Asian Republics. However needed or valuable your presentation might be to your audience, you cannot be forced into a position to foot the costs of the event so that they might be honored with your presence. I have http://www.skype.com

178

done such presentations via YouTube video or Skype when it was neither time-efficient nor financially effective to appear in person.

To fly for 40 hours, give a presentation the next day and immediately return, is not something that I am willing to do. It makes a huge difference if you are doing such things at age 27 or 72.

Foreign Social Obligations

In many cultures, China, Russia and Japan for example, business dealings are often started with drinking some of the worst distilled spirits known to man. Chief among these is what is known as "Chinese White Spirits."

This is the most commonly consumed distilled spirit in the world, and it is invariably trotted out when visiting dignitaries from European and American companies come to China. This is the most terrible, disgusting, vile, evil, and wretched potable liquor known to man.

Chinese White Spirits has the delicate taste of organic solvents that have been used to marinate piles of used Deasil engines and carefully filtered to make a clear white liquid with sufficient surface tension to form bubbles on the surface. Its smell is like a cat three weeks dead.

In polite society it is brought out with great ceremony in a fancy bottle contained in a silk-lined box adorned with gold cord. It is carefully poured into tiny glasses with thimble-sized cups. In not-so-polite-society in China's industrial north, they give you a water glass of this junk.

Then the toasting starts. Each representative gives a toast to honor every member of the distinguished visiting delegation. Their First Vice President of Production toasts your First Vice President of Production. Their First Vice President of Sales toasts your First Vice President of Sales – and so on. At every toast everyone is encouraged to drink up.

As the evening progresses the details of the proposed business deal is discussed. Our Chinese hosts are replacing their members with fresh late arrivals, who are again toasted. In the meantime the visiting delegation is starting to turn a bit green at the gills, and there is often a bet among the Chinese as to who will toss their cookies first.

At about the two-hour mark the Europeans and Americans are ready to agree to about anything to get out of there, even though the refreshed Chinese group is still going strong. The first meeting of the morning is, of course, at 8:00 AM, following a traditional breakfast of seafood soup featuring sea urchins and chewy octopus bits with appropriate sea weed and octopus-ink ginger sauce.

Sick, hung over and almost not able to see, the honorable and distinguished delegates from Europe and Asia are willing to sign almost anything to get out of their before another round of drinking begins to celebrate the successful conclusion of negotiations.

As they leave from the Beijing Airport, they are informed by the clerk at the Duty Free Shop that Chinese White Spirits cannot be sold to U.S. Citizens because U.S. Customs agents will not allow it into the country.

If you go anywhere in Asia and are offered something that smells too long dead, say that you have taken a vow of abstinence, or promised never to drink again on your mother's deathbed or have a weak liver that further assaults with alcohol might kill, and avoid the dangers of Chinese White Spirits.

This avoidance will help preserve your health and perhaps prevent financially dangerous agreements. There are many oriental customs worth emulating, but ending your international business dealings by worshiping at the Porcelain Throne is not among them.

Chapter 17

Love Your Work and Live Longer

If you do what you love and love what you do, then you have a starter recipe for good health and a long life.

∞ ∞ ∞

It is counter-intuitive to speak of the health benefits of starting your own business. Most would-be
entrepreneurs think that the added stress of taking
on a new business venture would be detrimental to
one's health, rather than beneficial.

Once a person is 50 and older, age takes its toll.
There is wear on the joints, it is likely that you have
been seriously injured in some life event, things like
Type 2 Diabetes crop up, your eyesight is not as
acute, commonly there is some hearing loss, and with
increased age there is a loss of muscle mass and
strength. Some of these depend on your genetics, and
there is not much to be done about that.

However, maintaining a reasonable diet, exercise
(that horrible word) and being physically active can
significantly improve your well-being and physical
appearance.

The truth is that a sedentary life with little or no
physical activities is a fast-track path to a premature
death. Seen from a biological point of view, we

human animals are made to function – do stuff. When all you do is to vegetate on a couch, look at TV and eat, the predictable result is obesity, high cholesterol, diabetes, high blood pressure. and an early demise.

Although there is the "Americans with Disabilities Act of 2009," which encourages the employment of the disabled, companies want to hire individuals who appear healthy, rather than those with costly health problems that can impact job performance and employee costs.

An Epidemic of Loneliness

We will all someday die of something, and if you wish to prolong life the best way is to be doing something that keeps you physically active. In 2017 the CDC recognized what it called, "An Epidemic of Loneliness" that it considered third only to obesity and heart failure in causing the premature death of the elderly. Frequently this loneliness is caused by the death of a spouse and other close relatives which leaves those without work in a precarious mental state. It is no wonder that you will feel despondent.

I felt that way when my wife Thresa died of pancreatic cancer. Typical of the disease, she died almost a year after diagnosis. We tried chemotherapy and surgery, but neither was successful in extending her life more than a few months. This outcome was not all bad, in that we had the chance to say our goodbyes and plan for the end.

She died in her own house with me and her son beside her, as she wished. She did not want her last sights and sounds in this life to be those of an Intensive Care Unit with bells, clanging noises and the hubbub of people rushing around in a futile attempt to extend her life by a few more minutes. When her time came she was ready to go.

If this sounds dispassionate on my part, it was not. Thresa was the love of my life, and ten years later she still is. I loved and fondly remember the years we had together and am deeply disappointed that we did not have the chance to grow old together. Even now, I mourn her passing.

Avoiding Self-Medicating with Alcohol or Drugs

While the twin hits of losing my job and my wife within two years had nothing less than a devastating impact on me, I knew both the temptation and perils of alcohol and drugs. Even though I was a child of the 60s, I avoided drugs all my life. I was too fond of my pipe smoking to tempt yet another even more addictive habit. I had quit smoking before Thresa and I married, and I have not regretted that decision.

I still have some of my pipes as relics, but have not fired them up for decades. It took six months before the final cravings left me. Towards the end of that time I would dream about smoking, but finally even those dreams disappeared.

I always enjoyed a drink and consumed my fair share of beer, bourbon and whisky in my life. I even made my own homemade pear wine from the fruit of my backyard trees. After my second set of heart-stents I very largely stopped drinking. I take an occasional drink, but not the four or five every night that I usually did.

How Doing a Business that You Love Prolongs Life

There are two broad areas where starting your own business doing something that you love can extend your life. The first are the psychological benefits of being actively engaged in the larger world of commerce with meetings, trade fairs to attend, seminars to give, and face-to-face consultations where you give and gain insights into the human condition and how to make it better for others. The second are the health benefits obtained by keeping your body, the human animal, functioning properly so that it can minimize the inevitable impacts of aging as long as possible.

Psychological health

A Hoveyism is, "There are few people so dull that I cannot learn something from or teach something to." As a consultant, lecturer, and presenter, I have learned to listen as well as speak. Within some passing comment can be the kernel of a significant business opportunity for the client, yourself or both.

When there is an embarrassing moment when your client asks, "Do you have or offer thus and such?" and you do not; that should prompt your own inner dialogue as to "Why don't I?" and "How could I?" Never be defensive about some skill you lack. If you do not have a skill, go get it, or contract with someone who does.

Being engaged in the concept of idea exchange puts you into a cooperative undertaking with other human beings at a level of mutual respect that falls very close to love. You will come to feel that this person is more like a relative, than just a business associate. You will feel glad to meet each other because you know that each such encounter will be filled with interesting interchanges on both a personal and business level.

You may develop joint ventures, partnerships, or virtual companies. The more frequent such exchanges are, the better you will feel about life, and you will reap psychological benefits. This is exactly like the bonding that takes place in combat units, among sports team members, and hunting buddies.

The alternative is the top down method of knowledge transmission such as in Grammar School. You are the expert, and your client knows nothing. This is disrespecting your client as a person. Somewhere, sometimes you will be wrong; and the relationship will be damaged when you are.

On the other hand, if the relationship is around

solving a problem and you are using your knowledge to guide your client to a better solution than he would have arrived at by himself, that is a much better place to be in the world of knowledge transmission.

Calculus of Successive Approximations

I view problem solving and the world's progression of knowledge in general as, "the calculus of successive approximations." With this approach it is acknowledged that there may be no totally correct or perfect solution to the complex problems presented by human existence. We strive, we get closer to a correct answer, but we will never achieve it. It is the ability to strive, to question what is supposed to be "known," and to seek the truth that makes us human and makes life worth living.

Perfection will never be achieved, but reaching for that goal is what keeps humankind stumbling along towards an understanding of our world and the part we play in it. Participating in some way in that search for knowledge, exchanging it freely, attempting to understand others and working together to solve pressing problems is psychologically rewarding and improves one's mental health.

We Are All Different

We are all differently gifted and afflicted. Sometimes, as in my case, this is the same thing. I have such a strong drive to be inventive that it motivates me to write, do videos, perform, speak, blog, etc. I cannot deny this creative impulse.

I call people like myself "Creatives." We often-times produce things in totally different fields and have an unusual ability to make correlations across knowledge platforms. I can look at a found object or a chance happening on the street and that can result in a new business concept or short story.

The ideas come so fast, that I cannot act on them all. Some I forget, other times I exorcise these intellectual demons by writing something or producing a video. If you are interesting in identifying such people, I did a presentation in 2015 in Zhengzhou, China, "Finding the Creatives in Your Corporation or Country." You may see a rendition of this presentation on YouTube at: https://youtu.be/eLGJaoBGa8w

Overcoming Life's Misfortunes

Sometimes losing one's job leads to a progressive cascade of evils which may include financial difficulties, losing one's home or divorce, which may arrive at the same time as the deaths of your parents. Such events piling on one after another, can give any reasonable person pause to wonder is life really worth living. Consulting a psychologist can help, but becoming interested in and starting your own business has numerous benefits for your mental health. These can include:

• There is pleasure in accomplishing a goal. When the world around you seems to give nothing but anguish, accomplishing even small tasks can be beneficial.

• Breaking business tasks into small steps. If you can divide a task into stages, even a large job does not seem the work seem so daunting. Here, for example, I am doing a book by writing it one chapter at the time. Each chapter finished and edited is a cause for a mini-celebration for which you can legitimately reward myself with a small intellectual or physical treat.

• Change from worry to planning. Switching from continually worrying about present problems to doing something creative with your business is mental relaxation and mental work at the same time. Your involvement in a difficult task with some personally significant payout helps beat back the steady drone of "Woe is me" thoughts.

• Desperate thoughts. Thinking about taking your own life, including detailed planning for the event, can dominate your thinking concluding with your ultimately making an attempt. If this is you right now, immediately seek professional counseling.

They may advise you to take on interesting work

tasks, including volunteering to do something to help others. These activities will dissipate suicidal thoughts as you will quickly discover there are many in the world who are worse off that you are; and what's more, you can help them in meaningful ways by expressing interest in them as individuals.

Your problems, whatever they may be, can be an asset. You are not the only one who has experienced depression, drug addiction or debilitating diseases. How you, and others that you know, got through this is a lesson worth spreading that can lead to a life-long vocation. People want to hear not only from degreed professionals, but from those they can identify with who have "walked the walk" and experienced their pain.

Physical Health

I have always been a hunter which requires walking through my woods, preparing food plots and retrieving and cleaning my game. This requires physical effort as well as giving me a psychological respite when I spend time alone in the woods.

Doing Something You Love to Get Exercise

If you are going to hunt or do other strenuous activities, always do so under a doctor's supervision. Before each hunting season I purposefully go on longer walks. When I walk to my hunting locations I may carry another 30 pounds worth of stands, guns and gear.

When I selected Hovey's Knives of China as my late-life business, a part of this was to provide a reason to do physical work, gathering wood for charcoal and pounding steel on an anvil, and grinding blades. I have videos of these processes on my Hovey's Knives of China YouTube Channel. A quick Google will find them as well as my hunting videos.

Sometimes Moderate Pain is Better than Medications

Age brings its challenges and the most recent for me was a claudication (blockage) of the veins in both legs. These made it tiring and painful to walk. From consults with my own physician and doctors at the VA, the only remedy was to keep using them to strengthen the formation of by-passing capillaries and take cholesterol-reducing medications.

Although progress was slow, their advice was sound and my ability to walk longer distances has steadily improved, although I can't do the 13-miles a day that I did when I was in my 20s. Pain medications, both over-the-counter and prescription medications where mine for the asking at the VA, but I resist taking them for fear of falling into the all-to-common addiction to opioids.

Temptations and Access to Opioids

During Thresa's year-long struggle which lead to her death, I administered a variety of strong pain medications to her, but did not take any myself. I never considered these recreational drugs. I had seen too many ruined lives that had resulted from addiction. I wanted no part of it. Some may have helped some of my symptoms from time to time, but the risks were not worth the danger.

For Thresa, who had a painful terminal illness that we all knew would play out in weeks or months, addiction was not an issue. Ultimately a drug mix was developed that largely eliminated the pain while still allowing her to communicate as she wished. She was conscious and mentally active to the very last seconds of her life.

Wellness Programs

Wellness programs at your local gym or hospital allowed me to go for regular exercises under supervision using a variety of equipment. If I needed my blood pressure monitored, that could be done in an instant. Devices on the treadmill let me reach and sustain a desired heart-beat level and progressively build up stamina.

This additional repetitive exercise also helped me lose weight, which had its own benefits in improving my health. From time to time I quit when I began to have those now-well-known-to-me symptoms of heart blockages. I had been down this road before and went to my cardiologists, who confirmed my suspicions.

Heart Disease

Heart attacks start taking their toll on people in stressful situations starting in their 40s and become increasingly common with age. Fortunately, the early detection and treatment of heart disease with stents and by-pass operations have extended many people's lives by decades, including mine. I have had one by-pass operation and a stent emplacement about 10 years later. I would not have survived these events had they taken place in the 1960s.

I did not have a classic heart attack, but felt a tightening in my throat with exercise. There are many other more subtle symptoms that can indicate heart disease include tiredness, shortness of breath, unexpected pains in the limbs and others. Even if you are doing reasonably well, a stress test is a prudent thing to do periodically when you are in your 40s and older, particularly if you are at risk because heart disease runs in your family, you had a history of smoking, or diabetes.

The recovery period after my second stent emplacement was more prolonged than the first and took months to recover, compared to weeks. This is when the claudication issues in my legs developed which at their most severe kept me from walking more than

100 yards without considerable pain.

This is the issue that I am working through now, and steadily recovering from. To all of us, age brings its junk with it in the way of unwanted diseases and mechanical failure of body parts like joints. Keeping physically active working at something that you enjoy and feel passionate about can bring pronounced health benefits.

Suggestions for Better Health

• Plan to walk and think. All I have to do is to walk out my back door, and I have miles of woods available to me. Most are not so lucky.

• Get an exercise machine. Use this repetitive motion to not only improve your muscles, but also to provide thinking time away from the distractions of everyday life and screen devices.

• Stop watching TV. Get your news from NPR or some other radio source to free up time for creative or physical activities which have you moving and thinking at the same time. When you want entertainment, buy inexpensive CDs or down-load from the cloud. That way you are in control to watch what you want when you want it.

I also use my TV for taking mind-expanding course work from The Great Courses which has audio content that you can listen to on your commute and video versions that you can watch on TV. If you like a particular TV series, you can purchase it and enjoy it, without ads, at your leisure.

• Have work partners. These can be either human or animal. Both have the advantage of making you keep to a schedule, doing regular activities, and provide a beneficial level of physical and social interaction.

When you are under canine supervision, for example, they will provide healthy interruptions as they will need to be fed, walked and generally looked after. I do not know of anyone who cannot smile at a pair of pups engaging in a game of tug-of-war or keep-away.

Dogs are different people. They have different personalities, physical traits, activity levels throughout life, and I find them to be enjoyable, compassionate, and protective creatures. For example, I have had my dogs spot rattlesnakes that I might have stepped on.

• Join a Wellness Program. There you can cultivate some friends as regular work-out buddies. This will encourage you to go. The same could be said of a bike-riding club, bowling team, or adult soft ball league. Do anything that gets you involved with other people while simultaneously providing physical exercise to keep the animal parts within you working.

• Start your own business. This is often an in-home project that cuts out the hours-long commute in your car. It is far more interesting a drive if you are a contractor and going to different job sites, but mind-numbingly boring if it is the same trip month after month. This commute, particularly in thick traffic such as in New York, L.A. or Atlanta, is mentally and physically draining and has a degree of hazard.

No one knows when a ladder will come off a contractor's truck and take out a tire so you have to cross two lanes of traffic to get to the shoulder of the road, while the world around you is passing at 70 mph, as happened to me.

I was lucky and except for a blown tire, I and my truck had no ill effects. Not having to commute is a health issue because it reduces the potential perils in your life and your daily stress level. Having a home-based business avoids that and provides days at the time when your car never moves out of the drive.

I hope I have sold you by this time that starting a new business, if it is appropriately chosen to your life stage, can have health benefits resulting in improvements in mind and body as well as your financial condition.

∞ ∞ ∞

About the Author

Born three days after the attack on Pearl Harbor and raised as a free-range child in a small Georgia town, Wm. Hovey Smith was raised in a literary environment. In the pre-TV era, there were always magazines such as *Time, Look, The Saturday Evening Post*, and *National Geographic* in the house as well as a daily newspaper which developed a deep desire write.

This desire was expressed in his writing for local and regional newspapers, self-publishing nine books, including four of the first ever published on AIDS, selling two outdoor books to New York publishers in the early 2000s followed by publishing his prize-winning titles, **Backyard Deer Hunting** and **X-Treme Muzzle-loading**.

Turning to business titles, he wrote the booklet, *Ideas For New Businesses in 2015* which was the springboard for **Create Your Own Job Security: Plan to Start Your Own Business at Midlife**.

Since writing does not always pay the bills, Smith

has had a diverse and wide-ranging professional career and started several businesses. As a teen he got his first job at Brown's Five and Dime.

He went on to earn two university degrees, served as a decorated combat Engineer Officer and became a Professional Geologist. Smith has also store clerked, owned a floral ship, founded Hovey's Knives of China, worked as an information scientist, a consulting geologist and as a business consultant to individuals and small businesses.

In addition he was also the producer of *Hovey's Outdoor Adventures* on **webtalkradio.net,** over 675 YouTube videos, a humorist, artist, knifemaker, outdoorsman and an international speaker on business topics.

The author has lived the life he writes about by having a variety of experiences including the arts, offering professional services, working for small and international companies, running his own companies, and facing life's challenges.

Index

Services Offered

On-Site Business Consultations

- Large group presentations outlining how to select the best opportunities for individuals.
- Smaller group meetings under potential business categories.
- Individual consultations to help select a person's most appropriate business opportunity.

Teleseminars

Individual Consultations

Bulk Book Sales

For additional information contact
Wm. Hovey Smith, at hoveysmith@bellsouth.net
createyourownjobsecurity.com
(478) 552-7455

www.ingramcontent.com/pod-product-compliance
Lightning Source LLC
Chambersburg PA
CBHW060237050426
42448CB00009B/1481